Leaping the Wall

Practical ways to empower faith
during difficult times

Julie Kloster

Copyright © 2012 Julie Kloster

All rights reserved.

ISBN-13:978-1478245032

ISBN-10:1478245034

DEDICATION

Dedicated to my dad, Richard Freeman, who taught me to write my first sentence, edits all of my work, and inspires me to believe that
by my God I can leap over a wall.
(2 Samuel 22:30b ESV)

CONTENTS

Acknowledgements

1 He Knows My Name (Message to Reader)

2 Beholding Glory

3 Is This Part of the Plan?

4 Altars of Remembrance

5 Waiting

6 Ever-Present Help

7 Choice and a Fallen World

8 Living in the Now

9 Grace Upon Grace

10 Peace That Passes Understanding

11 Sing For Joy; Dwell in Thanks

12 Hope

Final Note to the Reader

LEAPING THE WALL

ACKNOWLEDGMENTS

Special thanks to:

- My husband, Nate, and my daughters, Sarah, Chelsey, and Taylor—thank you for encouraging me to follow God's call on my heart.

- My parents, who first encouraged my love for the written word and believed in me even when I doubted. *I can do all things through him who strengthens me (Philippians 4:13 ESV).*

- My mother-in-law, Ardith, who demonstrates daily how to "leap the wall."

- Laura MacPartland, Melody Clinton, and Jane Pace, faithful first readers who offered honest encouragements.

- God, who has allowed me to be part of His work. I am so grateful. *Then the Lord put out his hand and touched my mouth. And the Lord said to me, "Behold, I have put my words in your mouth."(Jeremiah 1:9 ESV).*

He Knows My Name

"Rejoice that your names are written in Heaven."

(Luke 10:20b, ESV)

The greatest knowledge we can ever have is knowing God treasures us. —Francis Chan

My Story

God knew me before the world began. Before darkness hovered over the formless void that would become earth, before the protostars exploded in space and the sun and moon found their courses in the cosmic universe, before the waters of the earth teemed with living creatures, before the beginning—my name was written in God's book. Was it while the Spirit hovered over the surface of the deep that He first thought of me? Did He ponder for a moment as He penned my name to remember that my frame would be dust? Knowing my betrayals and self-centeredness, He still created me. He felt my grief and sadness and knew of the joys that would make me laugh and praise. This majestic king, enthroned in splendor, had a plan for my life before the foundations of the earth.

My name, deliberated over and decided with romanticism and sentiment by my mother, had long ago been written in God's book. Julie Ette. Some thought it unusual, named after Shakespeare's famous lover and my Great-Great-Aunt Ette.

Memories of Aunt Ette are vivid in my mind. When I knew her, she was tall and willowy with stooped shoulders. Memories of her laugh and her voice as she told stories and sang on the porch swing lilt through the passage of time. Aunt Ette and I baked cherry pies together. My tiny fingers pinched the edges of her famous crust next to her arthritic, veined hands gentle with demonstration and affection. Inheritance from her included a red streak of hair that I hear will be the first part to turn white if God allows me to live as long as she did. I wonder if she also had the unexpected spark of temper that I have always associated with that flaming streak.

Certainly Aunt Ette was much more daring and bold than I. Although her father owned much of the town, youthful Aunt Ette found adventure in stealing watermelons from the local farmer even though he would shoot at her while yelling curses from his back porch. She was the first woman to own a car in Minier, Illinois. After driving through her barn wall, she drove all the way to California. The dirt roads she traveled wound precariously through saw-toothed mountains and straight across long, hot deserts.

God's plan for Aunt Ette was intertwined with my life, and though she is now in Heaven with Him singing new, yet ancient songs, and embarking on fresh adventures, His plan for me on earth is still unfolding. Songs that Aunt Ette sang to me in the contralto voice that He formed initiated my love for music. Cherries that He grew filled the pies that she taught me to bake. The DNA that wound intricately together to form my red streak was planned by Him long before all of my hair fell out during the chemo days. He knows if I will live long enough for that streak to turn white like Aunt Ette's did. He knows it all.

Yes, long before Shakespeare wrote *Romeo and Juliet*, the story of the famous passionate lovers my mother romanticized about before naming me, God wrote my not-so-romantic name in His book. But I am loved more by God than Juliet ever was by Romeo. Each of us is loved with an everlasting love that stretches from eternity past to eternity future—endless, boundless, indescribable. A love that long ago inscribed my name in the Lamb's Book of Life, a book that prophesied not only my life with God, but the cross that would provide the only way for me to spend eternity with Him.

After my name was written in His book, ancient time passed. On the day that darkness reigned, and sorrow shrouded the earth with pain, my name was inscribed on the palm of His hands (Isaiah 49:16) where the nails declared that I was His. As Jesus breathed his last, stripped, scarred, and bleeding, He knew my name. He who for the joy set before Him endured the cross (Hebrews 12:2).

Was I part of the joy that He looked forward to? Is it possible that this God, as He died for me, looked forward to eternity with those He cherished? Knowing that His cruel suffering death was the only way for me to be with Him, did He provide it willingly so that I could spend eternity with Him in intimacy of fellowship? If I had been the only one on earth, is it possible that He would have died for me? Does He love me that much? He died in my place; my sins became His. My name had been written in His book from the foundation of time, and now another chapter of His will for my life unfolded as my sin was covered by His love poured blood. On that day, long before I was born, He redeemed my soul from the power of hell (Psalm 49:15).

Two thousand years have passed from that predestined, scandalous, yet glorious time. Genealogies formed. Cultures mixed. Continents were crossed. At the exact right moment, His plan for my birth was executed. He formed me in my mother's womb, cell by miniscule cell. He watched while the developing substance of my body cells formed tissues, tissues formed organs, organs formed organ systems, and organ systems formed the body that my spirit would inhabit for my lifetime. He numbered the hairs on my head, and He has never lost count of them, even through the chemo days when they brushed out in handfuls until eventually even I could count the number on my head—zero. All the days ordained for me were written in His book before one of them came into being. I breathed my first breath and began to fulfill His plan for my life. A plan for His glory and my good, God's Sovereign purposes for my life began to unfold.

Nothing in my life has surprised this God who knew me before time began. When my baby sister died, His heart ached and He watched as from my nearby crib I observed my parents weep in the pain of denial as they discovered their beautiful baby—pink rosiness drained leaving blood-pooled blue in her face.

As sorrows intermingled with joys, did He smile during the sun-kissed childhood days of daffodils and clovers, bumblebees, fried chicken in the park, and Gin Rummy on the floor with Grandma?

Did He hold my breaking heart when my parents divorced, engulfed with too much life sorrow and too little intimacy with the Comforter?

Surely He rejoiced with the angels when I finally heard Him softly calling my name, and I turned to follow Him for the rest of my life—twelve years old—alone no more.

Through dark years of adolescence and the joys of beginning my own family, He comforted and guided. When sorrow hit hard again with premature babies, miscarriage, tumors, cancer, and eye disease—He was my song in the night.

At what point did I realize that all of this—the joys—the sorrows—had purpose? None of it was accidental. That this Sovereign God didn't just stand by my side to hold my hand, but that He actually orchestrated the events in my life. He was intimately acquainted with all of my ways and each twist in the road of my life was intentional—drawing me nearer, strengthening my soul, and creating a desire within me to spend eternity with Him—all for the glory of His name.

He knit my body together in my mother's womb. That was the easy part. Knitting my soul to be unified with Him takes a lifetime that to Him is simply a vapor in the vast expanse of eternity. And on that day He will open the ancient book, and He will declare, "Her name is written in my book. Julie Ette Freeman Kloster. She is mine."

Message to Reader

My story is one small example of the sovereignty and love of God that began long before the world was created and stretches out to eternity future. Nothing that happens goes unnoticed by the God who forms every cell and counts every hair. The stories of God's sovereignty and love are interwoven throughout the chapters of this book just as they are interwoven through the pages of life. God's thoughts toward us are intimate and intricate in design. The foundations of faith that help us cling to Jesus during desperate times are embedded in each chapter. They are the cornerstone of our hope, joy, and peace. They are the solid beams that teach us to lean hard into Jesus remembering—waiting—trusting.

My hope is that this book will come alongside those of you who are struggling to cling to Jesus in desperate times. Its purpose is to journey with you as we focus on the heart of God who promises that He does all things for His glory and our good.

Many of you are going through hardships that I have never had to face. My sorrows compared to yours may be like gentle rain compares to a hurricane. I want you to know that I recognize this, and that my heart goes out to you, dear reader. I believe with all of my soul, however, that these Biblical truths apply to all of life's circumstances, no matter how desperate.

If I could, I would carry the mat where you lay wounded to the feet of the Savior. And that is exactly what I hope to do—to pick up a corner of your mat—and to carry you to Jesus—the one who loves you in ways you will never fathom—with an everlasting love that will not let you go.

King David passionately described the everlasting love of God that manifests itself in the sovereignty of the Almighty. The Psalms are full of David's meditations of grief and sorrow as he wept before the lover of his soul. Inevitably, as David poured out his heart before God, his eternal perspective changed, and his songs, etched eternally in the recorded Word, transpose from minor keys of sorrow to major keys of joy. David learned to abide intimately with the one who loves him to the depth of his being, and he declared his trust in the one who provides the grace and strength to overcome any obstacle.

In one instance, David expressed his deep trust in God who delivered him from his enemies. David proclaimed, *By my God I can leap over a wall. As for God, His way is perfect; the word of the Lord is proven; He is a shield for all those who trust in Him.* "For who is God, except the Lord? And who is a rock, except our God? God is my strength and power..."(2 Samuel 22:30b-33a NKJV).

Perhaps at the beginning stages of the chaos and horror, David was tempted to ask the same questions we often ask during times of crisis. Why didn't God stop the battle before it began? Where is God in all of this? As the battle raged, however, David felt God's presence in intimate ways, and out of that personal relationship with God, David sang songs of joy and praise to a God who didn't stop the battle, but was with him in the midst of it. At the end of the battle, David gloried in the understanding that the very battle that brought so much grief, sorrow, and loss also brought David closer to the heart of God.

This book explores the deeper questions of faith that haunt us. How can a loving God allow pain and suffering? How do sorrow and grief fit in with the biblical understanding that God has a good plan for our lives? Does God care about our pain? How, exactly, do we get to the point where our soul can declare with David, "By my God, I can leap over a wall?"

Further Investigation

At the end of every chapter is a section entitled *Further Investigation*. This section will provide further study options for you. Included is the name of a song that goes with each topic. You can search the internet using the title and find many different websites that will provide the song lyrics and an auditory recording.

A Bible passage is also included for further study. Ask the Lord to reveal His truth to you before you read it. The Holy Spirit's guidance unlocks mysteries of Scripture for those who truly seek Him.

The memory verse is provided so that in times of crisis you will have God's Word hidden in your heart. You will find that God brings these verses back to you when your fears and doubts are the darkest. God's Word is how He speaks to us today.

The reflective question is for you to search your soul. Use the spotlight of God's Word to search out the doubts and fears that harbor in your mind. You may choose to discuss it with someone else or simply ponder it in your heart.

Lastly, there is a prayer to help you ask God for application of His truth.

Scripture References

To differentiate exact quotes of Scripture from references to or paraphrases of Scripture, direct quotes are in italics. At the risk of breaking your train of thought, Scripture verses are included in the text for your reference so that you can easily look them up for study as you read, if you desire.

My prayers are with you, dear reader. It is an honor to come alongside you on this soul journey. My prayers for you claim the promise that He gives to all those who truly seek after Him.

. . . they should seek God, in the hope that they might feel their way toward him and find him. Yet he is actually not far from each one of us, for "In him we live and move and have our being"; . . . (Acts 17:27-28a ESV).

Further Investigation

Song: "He Knows My Name," by Tommy Walker

Bible Passage: Psalm 139

Memory Verse: *Do not fear, for I have redeemed you; I have called you by name; you are Mine! (Isaiah 43:1b NASB).*

Reflective question: How do you feel about the intimacy with which God knows each of us?

Prayer:

Everlasting God,

The vastness of the universe declares that you are a magnificent Creator! Yet in the grandeur of creation, you call me by name. You are intimately acquainted with everything about me. You know what I am going to say before I say it, and you know exactly the number of hairs on my head. You know me better than I know myself! Before I was born, you knew all about my life even to the day of my death. Your thoughts toward me outnumber the grains of sand. If I truly understood the depth of your love, my soul would be overwhelmed. I invite you to direct this journey of faith with me, Lord. Guide my thoughts as I read this book. Show me who you are. Amen.

Beholding Glory

Do not fear, for I am with you... Everyone who is called by My name, and whom I have created for My glory, whom I have formed, even whom I have made.

(Isaiah 43:5a & 7, NASB)

The whole world is charged with the glory of God. –Thomas Merton

The shadow of my tombstone loomed cold when I was forty-two. It was the first time I let my eyes behold the inevitable gaze of my death angel. My encounter with him dropped my shaking knees to the floor in prayer. I was in for a serious crisis of unbelief.

A spinal nerve tumor had obtrusively invaded the vertebrae of my backbone, shoving my spinal chord askew. It traveled ten centimeters alongside a nerve until it hung in dumbbell shape over my left lung. Surgery news was grim—eight hours of intricate nerve scraping and vertebrae removal that would land me in intensive care.

"Let me do this well, God," I prayed as I heard the diagnosis.

In preparation for surgery, I wrote letters to each of my daughters encouraging them to trust God no matter what happened. I sealed them with tears and gave them to my husband to deliver to my girls in case I didn't make it through surgery. By God's grace, my trust in God was solid; the crisis of unbelief came later. During eighteen months of painful recovery, my faith boat rocked.

Chronic pain deprives us of sleep and is fertile soil for dark thoughts and ravaged emotions. As I reflected on my mortality, doubts and fears set up residence. What if I was wrong about my faith? What if there was no God? What if I had believed a sham all along, and when I died I would just be one more corpse lying in the cold, cold ground returning to dust and forgotten by those who treaded above? As my soul searched for truth that I thought I already knew, God seemed silent for many, many months.

Questions haunted me. Their answers required trust in the eternal depth of the unfathomable ways of God. Why would this all-sufficient God create me? He had no need of me. Why would He place me on this sin-scarred earth knowing I would fail, weep, and hurt? And if He was truly a loving God, then why did He allow me to endure so much pain and suffering?

My crisis of unbelief was creating more suffering than any of my physical pain. It tormented my thoughts. For over a year I begged the Lord to take away my doubts, but they lingered long and hauntingly.

One day, the Holy Spirit spoke to me quietly in the whisper of his Word. "You were created for my glory, precious child. You were made for me." Head knowledge finally began to take root in my soul. God allowed what He did for His glory and the good of those who loved Him. He turned tragic events into passages of eternal significance: soul growth that brought His children nearer to His heart, salvation for those lost in darkness, longings for Heaven and home, and eternal rewards. All of these brought Him glory because they demonstrated who He is: our faithful, loving, Creator and our Abba Father, Daddy God.

Who can know the mind of God or fathom His ways? I don't know why this truth that I had known in my head for many years suddenly took root in my soul, but after seemingly endless dark days of searching and waiting to hear from God, I began to understand. Deeper understanding of God's truth began to set me free from the miry clay of doubt and fear. This allowed my soul to lift like eagle's wings soaring on the winds of truth—bringing joy. My vision of purpose in all of life, even suffering, began to clear.

Everything is for God's glory and the good of those He loves. All for a purpose—nothing insignificant or not seen—every detail allowed to be used to demonstrate who God is. When God is glorified, when we see Him for who He is and accept Him as our Lord and Savior, our souls receive the ultimate good that God has for us—an intimate relationship with our loving Abba Father, Daddy God.

Exalted honor, praise, or distinction accorded by common consent; something that brings honor or renown, a highly praiseworthy asset, adoration, praise, and thanksgiving offered in worship, majestic beauty and splendor, resplendence (*The American Heritage Dictionary of the English Language,* s.v. "glory."). These are all attributes of glory. And yet, God's glory is beyond human comprehension. There are no definitions that will adequately explain it. God's glory is who He is. When we bring glory to Him, we are simply pointing out His attributes. We declare who He is: love embodied; pure light; holy Savior; ever-present help; omniscient, omnipotent Father; and everlasting, faithful God. Glorifying God is a declaration: this is God—see Him, know Him, worship Him.

God's Glory in Creation

Creation's purpose is to bring God glory. It is indisputable evidence of the Creator. The Book of Romans boldly claims that anyone who sees creation and declares there is no God suppresses the truth. Since the beginning of the world, creation has declared God's invisible attributes, His divine nature, and His eternal power (Romans 1:20). Psalm 19:1 professes: *The Heavens declare the glory of God, and the sky above proclaims his handiwork (ESV).* Space telescopes beam back unfathomable, unsearchable images of God's glory. Brilliant hues of forming nebulas, vast galaxies, and supergiant stars that dwarf our solar system declare that God is beyond the scope of our comprehension. A spider weaving her delicate web, the rapid beat of hummingbird wings, an army of ants marching orderly, and the cells of the human body declare that God is the intrinsic Designer of the tiniest workings of life. Tsunamis, earthquakes, tornadoes, and hurricanes, with their destruction and devastation, declare the unmatched power of a mighty God.

The interdependence of life found in nature glorifies God, who ordains community and caring. Geese, guided by their Creator-designed instinct, flock together in V-pattern for thousands of miles and take turns leading so those who follow can fly in the draft with less effort. Bumblebees and hummingbirds gather nectar from the brightly colored bonnets of wild flowers and in the process of mutual symbiosis pollinate the plants which beautify prairies and pastures. Beavers build lodging that eventually dams up streams thereby creating meadows for deer and antelope to graze. The radiance of His glory is reflected in the detailed interdependence of life.

God uses creation to sooth our restless, tired souls by reminding us of our Creator. The song of a swallow, the caress of a cool breeze, and the flickering light of a firefly all declare the fragile delicacies of God's beauty. Sleepy dawn, peeking her head over the rim of the Grand Canyon, tosses aside blankets of shadow, reflects deep hues of color on carved canyon walls, and magnifies the creativity of the Creator. The setting orb over a pastel-reflecting sea declares the majesty of His beauty.

Meditating on God's glory demonstrated by creation promotes peace. Peace cradles and rocks our soul while singing lullabies about a God who reigns over all, a God who is bigger and more beautiful than our imaginations. The planets will spin in orbit, the sun will rise and set and the stars will shine until the Lord of all ordains otherwise. If God can keep the earth from catapulting into the far reaches of space, He can take care of me.

Though I am dwarfed by the grandeur of creation, in this entire vast universe, God chose to have a relationship with me. Humans are the created beings that God chose to commune with in intimate fellowship. We alone are created in His image. When we walk with Him, we reflect His glory, the very essence of the Creator of it all.

God's Glory in Miracles

Compassion is the heart of God. In the city of Nain, a widow was overshadowed by the mountains of suffering that formed the valley of the shadow of death. Her only son lay in a coffin being carried to its grave. When Jesus saw the widow, he felt compassion for her. "Do not weep," he said gently as he touched the coffin. Suddenly, the dead man sat up and began to speak. Imagine the mother's stunned silence and unbelievable joy. Jesus' compassion for this widow also unfolded an eternal purpose. Fear gripped the crowd that was following the widow, and they began to glorify God (Luke 7:11-17).

Scriptures abound with stories of miracles of God: healing of health and heart, bringing the dead back to life, supplying food in the midst of famine, parting seas, calming storms, and interpreting dreams and visions from Heaven. While each of these miracles was for the good of those involved, a greater purpose was also proclaimed—the glory of God.

Miracles abound even today. My daughter, Taylor, weighed one pound and thirteen ounces at birth. She was immediately whisked away by nurses administering CPR while a grim doctor pronounced her pessimistic prognosis. Taylor's life hung in the balance for months as I begged the God of compassion who healed the widow's son to heal my daughter. Today my premature child is a beautiful, talented musician who leads others in worship through music and the encouragement of her joyous personality and lilting laugh. Nothing is impossible with God (Matthew 19:26).

We live with other miracles every day: a child's first words, the opening of a rose, an accident prevented. Our lives are surrounded by miracles, but much like the crowds in Jesus day, we barely notice them for what they are—the workings of a loving God.

Sometimes the miracle is a miracle of the soul. Perhaps it doesn't result in the disappearance of our sorrow, but is found in the comfort of the Creator. God's ever-present help in suffering and His tender love cradle our breaking hearts and allow us to persevere in pain. His provision of the cross for our salvation and His plan for our future resurrection from the dead are the greatest miracles of all.

God's Glory in Suffering

I am the Lord, and there is no other, the One forming light and creating darkness, causing well-being and creating calamity; I am the Lord who does all these (Isaiah 45:6b-7 NASB).

When miracles happen, our souls rejoice with the cry, "God is

LEAPING THE WALL

good!" But miracles of healing aren't always given. Sometimes the cancer isn't cured, the accident isn't averted, or the premature baby dies. One family in our church didn't receive a complete miracle of healing when their son was in a car accident. He has spent that last decade in a wheelchair, unable to speak, though his mind is sharp. He and his family, however, testify of God's ever-present help and grace in all circumstances. "God is good—always," is their life's motto.

Tragedies can shake our faith, and deep in our soul we wonder, "If God loves me, then why does He allow so much pain in my life?" Surely, this heart cry is one of faith's greatest mysteries. We know from God's Word that He loves us immeasurably, that He is sovereign over all, and that nothing is impossible with Him. Why then, does He allow suffering?

Calamity is allowed by our Sovereign God for a purpose, but God promises that He does not afflict willingly to grieve His children (Lamentations 3:33). The Eternal Potter molds the horrific events that are part of a fallen world and recreates them for His glory and the good of those who love Him. God is sovereign over all creation. Nothing happens without His permission. Nothing is out of control. The Sovereign Creator reigns. Calamity grieves God's heart, and He is near to the broken-hearted (Psalm 34: 18), but He does allow pain and suffering for His glory and the good of our soul.

Suffering was part of God's plan for salvation. He created the world knowing Satan would introduce evil into the breathtaking splendor of Eden where Adam and Eve walked intimately with God. The way of the cross, a way of humiliation and suffering, was ordained by God the Father. Jesus cried loudly with tears, and He sweat drops of blood in the Garden of Gethsemane as He asked for His Father to remove His cup of torture. Yet, Jesus' agony was not removed.

Ultimately, Jesus trusted God's sovereign plan knowing God's ways were higher than His desires to escape pain. Jesus understood that God allows suffering for a purpose, and sometimes suffering is the only way for God to accomplish His purposes. Jesus learned obedience through what He suffered (Hebrews 5:8). Why would we expect less for our lives?

Part of the mysterious good that God works out of the suffering of Christ is that we know Jesus understands our suffering and pain. God became flesh; He was acquainted with sorrow and grief, and He died a cruel, torturous death. He has walked our road of humanity. And doesn't God use our suffering in the same way? Aren't we comforted most by those who have walked the same road of suffering before us because we know they will understand?

Personal privacy was important to a young woman at my church who was diagnosed with breast cancer. I barely knew her, yet she allowed me take her to her chemotherapy session. Since I was a breast cancer survivor, she believed me when I told her she would want a driver and someone to keep her company during the long sessions of intravenous drugs. She searched my face long and hard, and then she agreed. "Only you. I will let you do it because I know you understand," she explained. God's mysterious working of good in the midst of suffering allows us to comfort others in their heartaches and pain with the same comfort that God extended to us (2 Corinthians 1:4).

Is it not ultimately an issue of trusting that God will work the mysterious good that He promises? God, do I trust you enough to believe that you would only allow this in my life if it had some eternal purpose for your glory and my benefit? We might as well ask God the hard questions of our heart. He knows every thought before we think it and every word that is on our tongue before it is spoken. And if we listen intently, He speaks kindly, like a tender parent comforting a child:

> "*My son, do not regard lightly the discipline of the Lord, nor be weary when reproved by him. For the Lord disciplines the one he loves, and chastises every son whom he receives.*"
>
> *It is for discipline that you have to endure. God is treating you as sons. For what son is there whom his father does not discipline? If you are left without discipline, in which all have participated, then you are illegitimate children and not sons. Besides this, we have had earthly fathers who disciplined us and we respected them. Shall we not much more be subject to the Father of spirits and live? For they disciplined us for a short time as it seemed best to them, but he disciplines us for our good, that we may share his holiness. For the moment*

all discipline seems painful rather than pleasant, but later it yields the peaceful fruit of righteousness to those who have been trained by it (Hebrews 12:5b-11ESV).

Do I dare question this?

But I do dare. I dare to ask my Abba Father, Daddy God, "Is there no other way?" Even Jesus asked this in the Garden of Gethsemane. And gently my Abba Father comes to me. Gently like the whispering of the wind that Elijah heard in the cave of his despair (I Kings 19). My Abba Father takes me onto His lap. He wraps His majestic robes around my aching, tired body. He sooths my broken soul, and He sings over me lullabies of comfort from His Word. "My child, I am near to the broken hearted" (Psalm 34:18 NASB).

God used suffering and grief in the lives of Mary, Martha, and Lazarus to demonstrate His glory and to strengthen their belief in Him. Mary, Martha, and Lazarus were intimate friends of Jesus. He spent time in their home resting and being refreshed. Mary demonstrated her intimate love for Christ when she anointed His feet with oil, wiping His feet with her hair. Yet when Martha and Mary sent word to Jesus that Lazarus, *whom you love,* was ill, he did not come running as would be expected. Surely, Martha and Mary must have waited anxiously and expectantly for Jesus to hasten to heal Lazarus. Yet, Jesus delayed two days before He went to Martha and Mary. By that time the heart-broken sisters met Jesus with the news that Lazarus had died. And then Jesus gave them this unbelievable explanation—He had delayed on purpose. Jesus told the sisters, *"Lazarus has died, and for your sake I am glad that I was not there, so that you may believe" (John 11:14b-15 ESV).*

Yet even in this eternal plan, a plan to demonstrate Christ's power over death—an understanding essential to the belief of His followers—Jesus felt the grief of those He loved. Jesus did not miss their pain. When Jesus saw Mary and those with her weeping, He was so deeply troubled that He wept (John 11:33-35). Jesus did not weep because Lazarus was dead; He knew He was going to victoriously resurrect Lazarus. Surely Jesus wept because of the grief and sorrow of those He loved, and because of the suffering that was caused by the ravages of sin on a fallen earth. He grieved that His beautiful creation was marred by the evil work of the enemy, and in this marring, humanity suffered. Jesus wept with Martha and Mary in their grief, for He felt their sorrow and suffering.

Yet, Jesus loved Mary and Martha enough to allow their pain—for God's glory—for the good of their faith. Out of this tragic circumstance that was turned into the miraculous intervention of raising Lazarus from the dead, many people believed in Christ. Later, when Jesus was resurrected from the dead—certainly they must have remembered Lazarus and known that through the name of Jesus Christ we could have victorious celebration over our final enemy, death.

God's Glory through Evil

How can we explain the evil in the world? What about murders, tortures, and holocausts? How can a good God allow them? When God allowed free choice in the Garden of Eden, He also allowed evil to enter. Yet even evil is used by God for His glory. Evil makes us long for holiness. God is the essence of holiness, so in our longings for good, we long for God.

God used the plagues of Egypt and the death of Pharaoh and his army in the Red Sea for the glory of His name. The purpose of the plagues was *so that you may know that there is none like me in all the earth (Exodus 9:14b ESV)*. When Pharaoh, who had enslaved and tortured the Israelite people, pursued them in the wilderness, God used the death of the Egyptians in the Red Sea for His glory. *"I will be honored through Pharaoh and all his army, and the Egyptians will know that I am the Lord" (Exodus 14:4b NASB)*. God will do what it takes to proclaim His name throughout the earth and to bring us to himself.

After the crossing of the Red Sea, the tracing of God's hand could not be missed. The suffering the Israelites had endured was no longer foremost in their minds. Moses and the Israelite people began to see the goodness of God—His leading, His compassion, His rescue and deliverance. They began to sing songs of praise to the Lord. They recognized God was their strength. They praised His majestic power and holiness, the greatness of His excellence, and the loving kindness of a God who would lead His people to redemption. As Moses recounted the entire story to his father-in-law, Jethro, Jethro rejoiced in the goodness of the Lord and proclaimed, *"Now I know that the Lord is greater than all the gods" (Exodus 18:11a ESV).* The Israelites recognized God for who He was, and in that recognition, God was glorified.

God's Glory in Salvation

I, even I, am the one who wipes out your transgressions for My own sake, and I will not remember your sins (Isaiah 43:25 NASB). Even our salvation is ultimately for God's own sake, for the sake of His glory. Salvation provides the only way for His people, precious masterpieces who are workmanship created in Christ Jesus, to be with Him forever (Ephesians 2:8-9). Our salvation is so that God, perfect in holiness, can spend eternity with us. As a mother hen gathers her chicks under her wings, God longs to gather us to himself (Matthew 23:37).

Our salvation glorifies God's mercy, grace, holiness, forgiveness, compassion, and faithful love. He saved us so that we could demonstrate the complete beauty of His masterpiece in the fulfillment of the purpose of His workmanship. We become all that He created us to be—holy, blameless, forgiven and purified by the blood of the Lamb.

Whips, abuses, nails, thorns—all were part of God's plan of salvation for His own glory. By our salvation God declares who He is. He is the great *I Am*. The only way for us to be saved is through Him. He took the punishment we deserve. *I Am* is the only one holy enough to take away our sins. We are created for God's own glory—to honor Him, to worship Him, to love Him. And in this honor and love, we find our only true good.

God's Glory as our Focus

If our purpose is God's glory, then whatever we go through has eternal significance. The Apostle Paul was well acquainted with the cruelties of life. He explained:

> *Five times I received at the hands of the Jews the forty lashes less one. Three times I was beaten with rods. Once I was stoned. Three times I was shipwrecked; a night and a day I was adrift at sea; on frequent journeys, in danger from rivers, danger from robbers, danger from my own people, danger from Gentiles, danger in the city, danger in the wilderness, danger at*

sea, danger from false brothers; in toil and hardship, through many a sleepless night, in hunger and thirst, often without food, in cold and exposure (2 Corinthians 11:24-27 ESV).

Every lashing, every accusation, every cold prison floor brought new opportunities for Paul to glorify his Lord. Paul was very aware of his purpose in glorifying God in all circumstances.

When Paul and Silas were beaten and thrown into prison with their feet locked in stocks, they prayed and sang hymns of praise to God. The other prisoners were likely confounded as they listened. Suddenly, God shook the prison with a great earthquake. This demonstration of faith and God's power led to the salvation of the jailer and his entire family (Acts 16:23-34). Paul and Silas didn't fully understand God's plan as they were tortured for their faith and thrown into prison, but they trusted God, and He was glorified through them.

When we face difficulties in life, can we recognize that it has passed through God's hand and see it for what it is—an opportunity to bring glory to the Everlasting God? When we realize it is not random chance or bad luck, when we rely on the strength of the Holy Spirit, God can enable us to fulfill the purpose of every difficulty. We are God's witnesses (Isaiah 43:12). When we endure and stand strong, the proof of our faith, which is more precious than gold which is perishable, will bring Christ Jesus praise, glory, and honor (1 Peter 1:7). When we realize that all of life is for God's glory, then even our sorrow and suffering has purpose.

Further Investigation

Song: "Glory to God Forever," by Vicky Beeching

Bible Passage: Isaiah 43:1-13

Memory verse: *Be exalted, O God, above the Heavens! Let your glory be over all the earth (Psalm 57:5 ESV)!*

Reflective question: How can we be purposeful about glorifying God in every circumstance of our life? Make a list of practical examples.

Prayer:

Sovereign God, Lord of all Creation,

Help me to trust your sovereign will for my life. I claim your promise that you work all things for the good of those who love you and are called according to your purposes (Romans 8:28-30). Let every part of me reflect your glory, goodness, mercy, and love. May my life be a living sacrifice to you for the sake of your honor and glory both now and forevermore. Amen.

Is This Part of the Plan?

. . . the Lord your God turned the curse into a blessing for you, because the Lord your God loved you.

(Deuteronomy 23:5 ESV)

When we cannot trace God's hand of purpose
we must trust his heart of love. –Anne Graham Lotz

Broken shards of glass from the ceiling fixture scattered across the mahogany floor as the globe from the ceiling light crashed to the ground at my feet. As I stooped to pick up the dangerously sharp fragments, they began to levitate. Fragment by fragment prisms of the shattered glass floated through the air all around me coming together in puzzle-like fashion above my head. In orchestrated patterns they created a dazzling chandelier with each piece of fractured crystal refracting various hues of rainbow colors in myriads of directions.

I awoke from a very strange dream.

Symbolism hung heavily in the drowsy atmosphere like a cloud. I prayed. Analogy emerged from the fog of my sleepy brain.

The ceiling light globe seemed to symbolize my life. The broken pieces were expectations and hopes shattered by poor health—

seemingly irreparable slivers of glass that could never be put back together. Yet nothing is impossible with God, and His invisible force recreated the sharp, painful, brokenness into an object of breathtaking beauty. Each chandelier piece refracted light in hypnotic rays of color that wafted in various angles casting light and beauty in more directions than the single globe ever had. The Potter was recreating a masterpiece out of the unsalvageable. I pondered. The light source and power represented God. The light didn't come from me, but rather my purpose was to reflect the light. Each piece of brokenness reflected a before unseen characteristic of the beautiful light within. God was working glory and good out of disaster. My disaster.

Another surgery. This would be my fourth in five years. I never expected a major health breakdown in my forties; I came from a long line of relatives whose good health continued well into their eighties and nineties. My great-grandmother lived to be one hundred four years old—glorifying God until the day she died.

This fourth surgery was to prevent legal blindness. Medication to cure my breast cancer had created a macular hole in one eye first then the other. Central vision was distorted. I knew the treatment plan—lying face down for ten days while a gas bubble placed in my eye floated upward to press closed the hole in the retina. I also knew that while I was so grateful for the treatment, my vision would have some amount of distortion in each eye hereafter, even with the corrective surgery. Could God really work something good out of this? Though I shed many tears while facing the reality of my *new normal* or less than 20/20 vision, my heart harbored a peace that passed understanding. I had a deep knowing, anchored in my soul, that God would work His *good* out of even this. His transformation had already begun. My physical vision would be fuzzier, but my spiritual vision would grow stronger.

How often do I have spiritual macular holes? Do I even notice when my spiritual central vision is distorted? How often do I miss what God is doing because there is a gaping hole of darkness in the center of my spiritual retina that keeps His light from creating the correct image in my brain? Lord, give me the faith to see the unseen. Will I ever understand why you allowed my vision to be permanently marred? Probably not. Perhaps by closing the macular hole, you are also closing the spiritual holes of darkness in my soul—pressing hard against the gap—allowing the light to reflect in my life like it should—creating images of your glory that are no longer marred and distorted.

Nothing Good Withheld

No good thing does he withhold from those who walk uprightly (Psalm 84:11 ESV). Logically, if God does not withhold good from His children, but He does not always answer our prayers in the way we desire, then the answer we desire is not good for us. Understanding this helped me to realize that surrendering my will to God's will was not only required obedience, but was for my ultimate good. Pursuing God's will more than I pursued my own hopes and dreams meant I must put my trust in my Abba Father, Daddy God—knowing He would do what was for my ultimate good, even when I didn't understand. When the desire of our heart is God's will, our heart's desire will always be fulfilled. *Delight yourself in the Lord, and he will give you the desires of your heart Psalm 37:4 ESV).*

So how does this apply to the really hard stuff? What about cancer? What if I ask to be healed from cancer, but God does not heal? Would suffering with cancer actually be for my best good? The surprising answer is, "Yes!"

God cares about our souls much more than He does our physical, temporal bodies. Life on earth is fleeting. God says our time on earth is like withering grass on a sun-scorched summer day or like a vaporous mist that vanishes into thin air. Here today—gone tomorrow. But our souls are eternal and precious to God. Our earthly bodies groan and are burdened. But one day these mortal bodies will be swallowed up by *life* (2 Corinthians 5:4 NASB). True life—eternal life—life with God.

God allows earthly pain to promote soul growth. He desires souls that are knit with their Savior in dependence and intimacy so that eventually we become a reflection of God himself. God uses everything in our lives for good. And our ultimate good is to be conformed to the image of His Son (Romans 8:29). Even cancer can be for our ultimate good. What about the last enemy, death? When we belong to Jesus, physical death is the gateway to eternal life. A life with no more sorrow, no more pain, no more tears, no more suffering. We will be in the presence of our dear Savior forever.

Abundant Good

And we know that for those who love God all things work together for good, for those who are called according to his purpose (Romans 8:28 ESV).

Sold into slavery by his brothers when he was only seventeen years old, Joseph's life as a privileged son ended abruptly. Joseph's soul was in deep distress as he pleaded with his brothers to release him from the captivity of the cistern where they threw him like a discarded bucket. From the cistern, Joseph's brothers sold him into slavery. The evil jealousy that controlled his brothers kept them from listening to Joseph's desperate pleas for release.

Through heartache, sorrow, and physical abuse, Joseph was never alone. God was with him and prospered him through years of slavery and imprisonment until Joseph's distressed soul knit so closely with God's Spirit that Joseph could even interpret the dreams of others by God's power.

Years later, when Joseph was a ruler of Egypt, God's grace allowed Joseph to forgive his brothers and care for them when they came to him begging for provision during famine. Joseph then realized that even the evil plot of his brothers was part of God's plan for his life. Joseph's brothers must have been completely astounded at the depth of Joseph's forgiveness and faith when Joseph told them:

> *And now do not be distressed or angry with yourselves because you sold me here, for God sent me before you to preserve life. . . . And God sent me before you to preserve for you a remnant on earth, and to keep alive for you many survivors. So it was not you who sent me here, but God (Genesis 45:5 &7-8a ESV).*

Can I see this in my own life? Do I see a God who orchestrates good out of evil and suffering? Do I trust His plan?

My children were ten, thirteen, and sixteen when I was diagnosed with cancer. My deepest fear was leaving them motherless. Could I trust God even for that? Prostrate on the floor with face down and hands open wide, my physical prayer posture demonstrated what I wanted my heart to do, to release my will to God. Could I trust that if God called me home, that was what was best for my girls? Could I believe that he would rock them to sleep at night, listen to their cries, and provide for their needs if I were gone? Did He truly love them more than I did? Releasing my girls to God was the hardest thing I had ever done in my life. Could I truly believe that God would bring abundant blessing for my girls, out of cancer—even if I died? Psalm 27:13 has never meant more to me than at that time. *I would have despaired unless I had believed that I would see the goodness of the Lord in the land of the living (NASB).* Somehow, God would use this for good in the lives of my girls.

When we love God, abundance will always be our outcome. That abundance may not be seen until eternity, but God's promise for good will always be fulfilled. I clung to passages from the Bible that promised blessings and strength for each day. The eyes of my soul began to sharpen their focus on the eternal good promised in Heaven. *Passing through the valley of Baca* [weeping], *they make it a spring; the early rain also covers it with blessings. They go from strength to strength; every one of them appears before God in Zion (Psalm 84:6-7 NASB).*

God's Purpose for Us in Our Generation

. . . for you have done wonderful things, plans formed of old, faithful and sure (Isaiah 25: 1b ESV).

Each of us has a purpose in our own generation (Acts 13:36). God appoints our time on earth and the boundaries of our habitation with the purpose for us to seek Him and find Him, though He is never far from each one of us (Acts 17:26-27). When life seems out of control, we wonder if the pain we are going through is part of God's plan. God says He has made everything for its own purpose. Even wicked days full of evil are used by God to fulfill his purposes (Proverbs 16:4).

Queen Esther's life is an example of this. Esther's story is one of repeated tragedies: orphaned at a young age, raised in exile, taken into the king's palace against her will, forced to live in a harem. In the midst of this spiraling chaos, God had a plan for Esther to save her people from annihilation. First, though, Esther had to come to a complete surrender of her will and life to the Sovereign God.

Mordecai, Esther's guardian cousin, recognized the hand of Providence in Esther's role as queen, and he counseled Esther to seek mercy for her people who were slated for annihilation. In order to do this, Esther had to confront her husband, the king, who was known for his rash and harsh treatment of his former wife, Queen Vashti. When Esther protested this plan, fearing for her life, Mordecai proclaimed:

> *"Do not imagine that you in the king's palace can escape any more than all the Jews. For if you remain silent at this time, relief and deliverance will arise for the Jews from another place and you and your father's house will perish. And who knows whether you have not attained royalty for such a time as this?" (Esther 4:13b-14 NASB).*

Esther courageously followed the plan God had ordained for her. She asked her people to fast and pray, and then she trusted herself to her Sovereign Father. *"...I will go in to the king, which is not according to the law; and if I perish, I perish." (Esther 4:16b NASB).*

God turned the trauma of Esther's life into a plan of salvation for His people. Esther was the queen, and her beloved Mordecai became second only to King Ahasuerus. This gave Mordecai a position to promote the welfare of the Israelite people and the nation in which they lived. Amidst terrible hardship, fear, and suffering, God had a plan for Esther and her people that would result in their good and His glory.

When chaos appears to reign, we need to ask the God of grace to give us a heart like Esther's. Such a heart is willing to follow God no matter what the cost. Such a heart proclaims God's goodness regardless of the situation. Truly this is a genuine heart of faith, a heart that believes God will work out all things for our good, even when we do not understand His ways.

My friend, Carrie, has a heart like Esther's. She has a son who has profound impairment both mentally and physically. He lives in a special home that is well-equipped to meet his needs. One day I asked Carrie to share her story with me. She hesitated, and her eyes filled with tears. "Stephen's birth was a watershed for me," she said. "It has been hard. Really hard." She paused and took a deep breath. "I guess, I just got to the point that I realized I have to trust God no matter what."

There is no doubt that God has a purpose for her son, Stephen. Stephen's life impacts people in his generation. His smile lightens the mood of everyone near him. Though we will never understand why Stephen was born with such severe disabilities, God did not make a mistake with his birth. On this earth, my dear friend, Carrie, will always bear the pain of sorrow. But one day—one very special day—one day when Carrie and Stephen have reached the other side—all will be restored. Stephen will run, and laugh, and tell Carrie the details of how Jesus wrapped himself around Stephen during his years on earth—years that compared with eternity are just a whisper in the wind.

God's Protection of Our Soul

Often followers of Christ proclaim God's protection of His people. Yet, Carrie's story is proof that God does not always protect us from physical harm. What exactly does God promise to protect? God is the protector of our soul. *The Lord will protect you from all evil; he will keep your soul. The Lord will guard your going out and your coming in from this time forth and forever (Psalm 121:7-8 NASB).* God will do what it takes to protect the souls of those who belong to Him.

Sometimes, protection of our souls includes hardship and sorrow. Remember, God is about our soul growth—that which draws us nearer to Him. David recognized this and proclaimed . . . *in faithfulness you have afflicted me (Psalm 119:75b ESV).*

God protects our soul by His very presence and comfort in the midst of every situation. David penned these thoughts well:

> *. . . if it had not been the Lord who was on our side when people rose up against us, then they would have swallowed us up alive, when their anger was kindled against us; then the flood would have swept us away, the torrent would have gone over us; then over us would have gone the raging waters. Blessed be the Lord, who has not given us as prey to their teeth! We have escaped like a bird from the snare of the fowlers; the snare is broken, and we have escaped! (Psalm 124:2-7 ESV).*

Does this mean that God never protects us physically? God's eyes are always on His children. He has ordained prayer to be part of His work, and His Word tells us to bring our heart's requests to Him. God sends His angels to protect us all the time. In fact, if we have prayed for protection, and our prayers are not answered in the way we want, we must trust that God has a good reason for allowing whatever comes. "When we cannot trace God's hand of purpose, we must trust His heart of love" (Lotz). God's heart of love is found in the fact that *he does not willingly afflict or grieve the children of men (Lamentations 3:33 ESV)*. If God has allowed it, we can trust that it has purpose.

Remaking the Pot

What if our sorrows are the consequences of sin? Does God work good results out of even sin? Jeremiah shared a beautiful illustration of God's sovereign remolding of our lives. *So I went down to the potter's house, and there he was working at his wheel. And the vessel he was making of clay was spoiled in the potter's hand, and he reworked it into another vessel, as it seemed good to the potter to do (Jeremiah 18:3-4 ESV).*

We are the pot formed by God, the Potter. He molds us into the image of His Son. When sin ruins the beauty that He is creating, He reshapes our lives, yet continues to transform us into the image of His Son.

The next question that comes to mind is addressed by Paul in his letter to the Romans. *What shall we say then? Are we to continue in sin so that grace might increase? May it never be! How shall we who died to sin still live in it? (Romans 6:1-2 NASB).* God's mercy does not give us license to continue in sin. True followers of Christ desire to be like Him. Hearts that truly love God desire His ways and are appalled at the thought of grace being a means to allow sin. A heart bent on its own desires is not a heart that seeks after God.

Still, all of us are human and fall short of the glory of God. In fact, the closer we move to the light which is Christ, the more we recognize the darkness within us. Keeping short accounts with God by repenting as soon as we recognize the sin within us is part of the plan to mold us into all that He wants us to be.

Though God uses even our failings to shape our lives, sin does produce consequences that can be horrifically painful. Sometimes these painful consequences last an entire lifetime. This was true for King David. Taking advantage of the honor of kingship, David committed murder and adultery. Yet, God said that David walked before Him in integrity of heart and uprightness (I Kings 9:4). Despite David's sin, he had right standing before God because he confessed his sins and received freeing forgiveness. Still, David had a lifetime of painful consequences that played out in the lives of his children and David's relationship with them. Indeed, had it not been for David's intimate walk with God, the consequences of David's sin would have been too great for him to withstand.

A contemporary story of hope rising from the despair of sin is the ministry of Charles Colson. As special counsel for President Richard Nixon from 1969 to 1973, Chuck Colson was one of the Watergate Seven who pleaded guilty to the charge "Obstruction of Justice." Pressures from the Watergate scandal brought Colson to a point of repentance, and he accepted Christ as his Savior shortly before he was sent to Maxwell Prison in Alabama. Upon hearing about his conversion, the *Boston Globe* commented, "If Mr. Colson can repent of his sins, there just has to be hope for everybody" (Prisonfellowship.org).

As a new follower of Christ, Colson used his prison experience to begin the ministry *Prison Fellowship*. The following story recounts Colson's first thoughts of this ministry:

> One day, shortly before leaving prison, Colson was going about his business in the prison dorm while some inmates played cards. Suddenly, one of the players, a six-foot-tall prisoner named Archie, bellowed, "Hey, Colson. You'll be out of here soon. What are you going to do for us?
>
> Suddenly, the whole room fell silent. All ears were straining to hear the answer. "I'll help in some way," replied Colson. "I'll never forget you guys or this stinking place" (Prisonfellowship.org).

Colson's ministry angles include befriending children who have a parent in prison, a reentry program to assist released prisoners to live a reformed life, and in-prison outreach programs among others. Colson is a living example of how God uses even the consequences of our sin to transform lives into lives that shine for His glory and the good of His people. When sin tempts us to despair, we remember the mercy of God who will be faithful to complete the work He began in us (Philippians 1:6).

No matter what we go through, God is with us. He orchestrates the events in our life for the good of our soul. God is eternal, and the work that He desires in us is also eternal. God will allow what it takes to knit our souls to Him. He cradles our heart, protects our soul, and allows enough pain in our lives to create a longing for Him and our celestial home. God causes all things to work together for the good of those who love Him and are called according to His purposes (Romans 8:28).

Further Investigation

Song: "Blessings," by Laura Story

Bible Passage: Book of Esther

Memory Verse: *And we know that God causes all things to work together for good to those who love God, to those who are called according to His purpose (Romans 8:28 NASB).*

Reflective question: What hardship in my past has God already used to draw me nearer to himself? Share your thoughts with a friend.

Prayer:

Abba Father, Daddy God,

When I do not understand your ways, help me to trust your heart. Impress upon my soul your everlasting love. As a child clings to the hand of a trusted parent when frightened, I cling to you. Your ways are higher than mine. Please give me the grace and faith to believe that you will work out all things for the good of my soul. Help me to trust that nothing is allowed in my life which has not passed through your hand of love. Amen.

Altars of Remembrance

O my God, my soul is in despair within me; therefore I remember You...

(Psalm 42:6 NASB)

'Memory' labels a diverse set of cognitive capacities by which we retain information and reconstruct past experiences, usually for present purposes. Memory is one of the most important ways by which our histories animate our current actions and experiences.–John Sutton

A small basket placed on my daughter's dresser is enfolded with lace and pink ribbons; it is an altar of remembrance. Inside the basket are three carefully placed items. The first is the blood pressure cuff specifically made for premature babies. It measures six inches in length and one inch in width. The second item is the knitted cap that my daughter, Taylor, wore the day she was born. The multicolored yarn had covered her head down to her ears to help her retain her body heat. It would also fit snugly on a small orange—the size of Taylor's head at birth. The third item consisted of two four inch squares of gauze that were folded together to form a diaper; even the manufactured diapers made for premature babies were too large for her. My altar of remembrance contains the physical reminders of the miraculous birth of my daughter.

Prayers of gratitude swell as I trace the basket ribbons and gaze at my sleeping beauty. Finally home from the hospital and freed from the burden of machines, Taylor sleeps peacefully in her crib. She is breathing freely without respirator or oxygen. She is three and a half months old, yet I marvel at how big she seems at only five pounds—more than double her birth weight of one pound thirteen ounces. My fingers gently trace the scars on her neck and leg. These scars will be lifetime reminders of the medical interventions that God used to save her life.

Another altar of remembrance: scars on her skin and my heart—healed, yet tender.

Even today if I trace the scar on her neck, Taylor squirms, giggles, and pulls away. Memories flood back as I remember. The rush of the tsunami waves of fear that flooded in with each earthquake of news can still nearly stop my heart: collapsed lung, 100% oxygen, full respirator, high blood pressure, immature digestive system, eye disease, potential for brain hemorrhages, heart murmur, shock, infection. I experience again the strong rip currents of grace and mercy that engulf the fear, washing it into the ocean of the *peace of God, which surpasses all understanding,* when I surrender my will to the one who loves Taylor more than I do (Philippians 4:7a).

Altars of remembrance undergird our faith. When our soul is tossed in the storms of life like a ship on the high seas, we remember that our anchor is in the Rock of Ages. Throughout the Old Testament there are stories of altar building to worship and remember God. After the flood, Noah built an altar (Genesis 8:20). Abram build an altar in the location where God met him and promised that his offspring would inherit the land (Genesis 12:7). Isaac, Jacob, Moses, and Samuel are among those who built altars of remembrance. Placing a stone as an altar of remembrance, Samuel explained its significance when the Israelites battled the Philistines, *"Thus far the Lord has helped us."* (I Samuel 7:12 NASB). When Jacob built his altar at Bethel he proclaimed, *"I will make an altar there to God, who answered me in the day of my distress and has been with me wherever I have gone."* (Genesis 35:3b NASB).

Focusing on God is the foundation for altars of remembrance. When we remember who God is and what He has done in the past, our hopes rise on the winds of memory. God is the same yesterday, today, and forever (Hebrews 13:8). The same God who has helped generations in the past will help us today. His promises are sure and trustworthy, and they offer peace and hope for whatever comes. When we remember God, fears subside, faith is fortified, and courage for the future is magnified.

Remembering the God of Ancient Time

During difficult times, it is important to remember that our God is the same God of ancient time. Scripture records God's faithfulness throughout history. This same God will meet us with the same compassion, faithfulness, and love that He has demonstrated throughout history. God's character never changes.

God is the Creator of all life. When shadows of darkness close in around us, we need to take time to reflect on the light of creation. Observe God's world; remember the Creator. Creation displays God's invisible attributes, His eternal power, and His divine nature (Romans 1:20).

When God spoke to Job out of the whirlwind of horrific grief that surrounded him, God drew Job's attention to creation as it displayed the knowledge and power of God (Job 38-42).

> *Where were you when I laid the foundation of the earth? Tell Me, if you have understanding, who set its measurements? Since you know. Or who stretched the line on it? On what were its bases sunk? Or who laid its cornerstone, when the morning stars sang together and all the sons of God shouted for joy (Psalm 38:4-7)? Or who enclosed the sea with doors . . . And I said, "Thus far you shall come, but no farther; and here shall your proud waves stop" (Job 38:8a & 11 NASB)?*

Before my daughter, Taylor, was born, it seemed to me that God was harsh when he spoke to Job. After all, hadn't Job lost everything? During the months that Taylor was in the hospital, however, I reread passages in Job over and over from a heart of loss, confusion, sadness, and doubt. As the Holy Spirit spoke God's living Word to me from the

Book of Job, His voice was firm, yet tender and comforting. God reminded me of His sovereignty, and He encouraged me to trust Him even when I didn't understand.

God's words to Job reminded me of how I spoke to my children when they were distraught. I could imagine how, as a parent, I would get down on my knees, hold my child's shoulders gently, and stare into her eyes trying to get her full attention. That is how I imagined God. He was my Abba Father, Daddy God, reminding me with care and compassion that He was still in control. God spoke to me with the same words that He had spoken to Job thousands of years before.

Throughout the Book of Job, God reminds us of who He is. Each morning dawn displays His faithfulness. God alone has entered into the springs of the sea and walked in the recesses of the deep; his knowledge is infinite. The immeasurable expanse of the universe displays His great power. Wind, storms, snow, hail, and floods demonstrate His unsearchable ways. New crops that poke through black soil and rains that fall verify His provision. Drops of dew, cell structures, and the intricate design of animal life confirm His attention to detail. His eternal power triumphs over the gates of death.

As I read through the Book of Job, God asked me the same question that He asked Job long ago, "Who are you going to trust?" God's implication seemed to be: "Julie, Julie—you are a mere human. You cannot understand my ways even if I tried to explain it all to you. You have to trust me. Remember—remember—remember who I am— Creator of all, Almighty in Power, Magnificent God."

In crisis, we also need to remember the deeds and wonders God performed in generations past.

> *I shall remember the deeds of the Lord; surely I will remember Your wonders of old. I will meditate on all Your work and muse on Your deeds. Your way, O God, is holy; what god is great like our God? You are the God who works wonders; You have made known Your strength among the peoples (Psalm 77:11-14a NASB).*

Scripture is written so that we can know God personally and intimately. The Bible stories of old are not mere history lessons, but stories of God himself. When we read Scripture, our focus shouldn't be on the people of the Bible, but on the God who sustained them. We ponder on their God—our God.

The same God of Adam, Abraham, Noah, and Daniel is our God today. The everlasting Father never changes. The Creator who designed paradise continues to create new life today. The Sustainer who gave Noah the perseverance to build an ark will give us the perseverance to complete whatever task He ordains for us. The Protector who saved Shadrach, Meshach, and Abednego from the fiery furnace can rescue us from the blazing infernos in our lives. The Great Physician who healed the blind, deaf and lame can heal us. The Comforter who met Elijah in the cave of despair will meet us in our depression. Jehovah Jireh (God our provider), who fed the 5,000, will provide for our needs. The Savior who has power over death will one day resurrect our heavenly body from the earthly tent in which we now live.

As we read through the ancient writings of Scripture, we remember God. The words are mysteriously alive. God is speaking to us today with spiritual applications about the detailed circumstances of our lives. The unchanging God of the patriarchs is the same God today. We have the same love, the same power, the same grace, the same strength available to us today in our unchanging, eternal God of love. God will meet us in the same way in our generation. Each of us has a purpose in our generation, and God will enable us to accomplish His call on our life, even when that walk seems dark, lonely, and long.

Remembering our ancient God emboldens our faith. The God of Abraham, Isaac, and Jacob is the Great *I Am*. He is a present-tense God. *I Am* here. *I Am* with you. *I Am* unchanging. *I Am* ever-present. *I Am* omniscient and omnipotent. *I Am* eternal. *I Am*.

Remembering God in My Life

Four months of bed rest gave me plenty of time to ponder and pray. This was my fourth difficult pregnancy. When my fears of miscarriage or premature birth loomed, I remembered God's faithfulness through the other pregnancies. My two precious daughters reminded me that God was a God of miracles and that despite the appearance of circumstance, He could save this child.

In between the births of my two daughters, however, I had lost a child. An apple tree in the back yard planted in her memory was an altar of remembrance. I remembered that if my worst fears were realized, God would see me through. It would be very painful, but I would receive God's all-sufficient grace and ever-present help. I found comfort in the verse that said He held my tears in a bottle and recorded them in His book (Psalm 56:8). This caring, compassionate God will one day wipe away all my tears of loss when I meet my child face to face in Heaven.

My past experience with God also helped me know that this child had a purpose in my life regardless of how long I carried her. My first loss had opened many doors for me to speak to other hurting women. It also helped me to remember to keep my hands open to the will of God. Not my will but yours be done—Christ's prayer in the Garden of Gethsemane.

Remembering how God has helped us in the past reminds us that He will be with us in the future. Whatever happens, God is already there. He helped us before; He will help us again. We look back and remember like Samuel did, "Thus far God has helped me."

Journal entries, stories, poetry, and songs of our walk with God are helpful altars of remembrance. After the Israelites safely crossed the Red Sea, Moses and the Israelite people sang a song led by Miriam. The women who danced joyfully led the celebration of praise. That song is recorded in Exodus 15 for all people throughout every generation to remember the goodness of God. King David recorded many psalms (or songs of praise) that glorified God as they detailed his life's journey. Jesus' mother, Mary, also recorded her faith journey as she recited the *Magnificat* which was filled with the remembrance of God as it quoted fifteen passages from the Old Testament about God's faithfulness (Luke 1:46-55). We, too, can create altars of remembrance by recording the working of God in our lives. These reminders serve as encouragement to our faith in difficult times. We remember: God has always been faithful; He will not fail me now.

Remembering how God has met us in the past also helps us trust God for the future. God promises that just as He has carried us from the womb, He will be with us to our graying years; He is the same always (Isaiah 46:3-4). We remember and proclaim with the psalmist:

> *God is our refuge and strength, a very present help in trouble. Therefore we will not fear though the earth gives way, though the mountains be moved into the heart of the sea, though its waters roar and foam, though the mountains tremble at its swelling (Psalm 46:1-3 ESV).*

Remembering the Character of God

When we meditate on the character of God, our souls are soothed and our faith is strengthened. Remembering who God is by meditating on individual attributes of His character is critical to building faith. Journey with me as we consider just as few of the inexhaustible characteristics of God on which we may meditate:

Meditating on the God of Comfort

Comfort, comfort my people, says your God (Isaiah 40:1). Comforting the souls of his people is the heart of God. His care is tender and gentle like a shepherd of young lambs. *He will tend his flock like a shepherd; he will gather the lambs in his arms; he will carry them in his bosom, and gently lead those that are with young (Isaiah 40:11).*

Sometimes a ewe is too weak or overwhelmed to care for her lambs. In these cases the shepherd will bottle feed the lambs until the mother is stronger. A good shepherd cradles the lamb in his arms while he coaxes her to take nourishment. Jesus is like that. When we are weak and worldly worn, He cradles us near to His heart and nourishes us with His presence. He whispers messages of encouragement and love through his Word.

When nursing ewes become stronger, the Shepherd gently retrains the ewes to accept again their young. Similarly, as we are strengthened by God's care, He gently guides us as a shepherd leads nursing ewes.

Meditating on God's Omniscience

God knows every detail of life. He has measured the waters in the hollow of His hand, marked off the Heavens by the span, calculated the dust of the earth by the measure, and weighed the mountains and hills (Isaiah 40:12). He numbers the hairs on each head (Matthew 10:30) and perceives our thoughts before we speak them (Psalm 139:2-4). His care is intimate, precise, and omniscient. God's eyes and heart are perpetually on His people.

Meditating on God's Wisdom

God is the embodiment of wisdom. He makes no mistakes. *Who has measured the Spirit of the Lord, or what man shows him his counsel? Whom did he consult, and who made him understand? Who taught him the path of justice, and taught him knowledge, and showed him the way of understanding (Isaiah 40: 13-14 ESV)?* God does what is best for His glory and our good, but we can never fully understand the unsearchable ways of God. We must trust Him like a small child trusts her father. We place our hand in His and let Him lead us, for He knows what is best. When we meditate on His wisdom, we more readily trust His plan.

Meditating on God's Sovereignty

Do you not know? Do you not hear? Has it not been told you from the beginning? Have you not understood from the foundations of the earth? It is he who sits above the circle of the earth, and its inhabitants are like grasshoppers (Isaiah 40:21-22a NASB). When we face various trials in life, we need to remember our sovereign God. He sees things we can never see, knows things we do not know, and has an eternal perspective that we can never grasp. When we question the purposes of God, we need to refocus and meditate on His sovereign, unsearchable, inscrutable love for His people.

God, who knows our heart and our every thought, reminds us that He is aware of every detail of our lives. He understands us better than we understand ourselves. He reminds us in the Book of Isaiah that He alone can give us the strength we need, for He is the sovereign God:

> *Why do you say, O Jacob, and assert, O Israel, "My way is hidden from the Lord, and the justice due me escapes the notice of my God?" Do you not know? Have you not heard? The Everlasting God, the Lord, the Creator of the ends of the earth does not become weary or tired. His understanding is inscrutable. He gives strength to the weary, and to him who lacks might he increases power (Isaiah 40:27-29 NASB).*

God's understanding of our emotions, thoughts, fears, and grief is inscrutable. He knows us better than we know ourselves, for He is our Creator. Nothing escapes His notice. He never sleeps or becomes weary of our troubles. When our friends are tired of hearing our story, God still wants to hear what is on our heart. He alone can give us the strength to get through whatever our circumstance.

Meditating on God's Faithfulness

Do not fear, for I am with you; do not anxiously look about you, for I am your God. I will strengthen you, surely I will help you, surely I will uphold you with My righteous right hand (Isaiah 41:10 NASB). God is with us every moment of every day. He faithfully offers grace and strength to fulfill every purpose to which He calls us. His help is ever sure; we need not ever doubt it. Meditating on God's faithfulness eases anxiety. He will never leave us nor forsake us (Hebrews 13:5).

I experienced the steadfast faithfulness of God when He called me back to teaching in the public schools after many years as a stay-at-home mom and freelance writer. The first year back was difficult, and I had to lean hard on God for wisdom and strength for each day. I knew this was a task I could not accomplish without Him. Some days were so difficult that I wondered if I had heard correctly God's call on my heart.

God met me faithfully every morning. The sun would peek over the horizon as I traveled through the country to the small rural town where I ministered to children, many of whom were hurting and broken. Sometimes a pink bolt of light would shoot straight up into the sky announcing the new day with fanfare and exuberance. Other days the horizon across frosted fields was hazy purple all around, sleepy dawn still tucked under blankets of night. On mysterious mornings, fog settled in long wisps across cornstalks, or it would crystallize on every branch of tree. Every unique, breathtaking sunrise reminded me that God's mercies were new every morning (Lamentations 3:22-23). These morning drives were interludes with my Creator offering intimate fellowship. I poured out my soul's heartaches for my students to the God who loved them more than I did. I told my Heavenly Father of my struggles with feelings of inadequacy in meeting my students' needs, and I asked Him to bestow wisdom and creativity so that I could help them to reach their potential and purpose.

Throughout each day, God wrapped himself around me, whispered encouragements, and fortified me for the purpose that He had designed for my students and me.

As the day ended, the sun would set as I traveled home. Its symbolism reminded me that God had faithfully guided me, just as He had promised.

Moment by moment, day by day, year by year, faithful to a thousand generations to those who love Him and keep His commandments is our everlasting God (Deuteronomy 7:9).

God's faithfulness is evident in the life of my ninety-four year old mother-in-law. "Great is Thy Faithfulness" is her favorite hymn. At thirteen years of age, her mother died, leaving her to be the maternal caregiver for six siblings. She felt God's call on her heart to drop out of school to assist her father in running the family farm. She grew and canned her own food, cooked for six brothers and the helpers on the farm, washed clothes without modern convenience, and shepherded the hearts of her siblings. To this day her baby brother, who would crawl into her bed every night and fall asleep with his hands on her cheeks, sends her a Mother's Day card.

Years later, God continued to lead and provide. When Mom's oldest brother married and brought a bride home to run the farm, Mom tested into college and received her degree from Moody Bible Institute. When WWII ended, her beloved sweetheart came home and together they raised eight children. Her life has been a life of dedicated ministry for her Savior. Many souls have been brought to Jesus through the love of this dear woman who leans on the faithfulness of God.

In recent years, a series of strokes has caused Mom physical and mental impairment, but when she hears her beloved hymn of the faithfulness of God, she closes her eyes in worship. She mouths the words, "Faithful, faithful God." She is living testimony of God's faithfulness. Her life reminds us that strength and courage are fortified when we remember that our Faithful God is with us wherever we go (Joshua 1:9).

Our God is a faithful God. He will neither fail nor forsake us. Jesus promises *I am with you always, even to the end of the age (Matthew 28:20 NASB).* His faithful presence empowers us to trust Him even in our darkest night.

Meditating on God's Steadfast Love

Frederick M. Lehman is the author of the beloved hymn, "The Love of God". The beautiful poetry of this beloved song describes the inexhaustible and infinite love of God.

"The Love of God"

Could we with ink the ocean fill,
And were the skies of parchment made,
Were every stalk on earth a quill
And every man a scribe by trade,
To write the love of God above
Would drain the ocean dry.
Nor could the scroll contain the whole,
Though stretched from sky to sky.

O love of God, how rich and pure!
How measureless and strong!
It shall forever more endure
The saints and angels' song.

Frederick M. Lehman, 1919

LEAPING THE WALL

This third stanza of the hymn was written on the wall of a patient's room in an insane asylum. It was this stanza that inspired Lehman to write the song. Lehman explained the lyrics of his beloved hymn in 1946.

> *One day, during short intervals of inattention to our work, we picked up a scrap of paper and, seated upon an empty lemon box pushed against the wall, with a stub pencil, added the (first) two stanzas and chorus of the song . . .Since the lines (3rd stanza from the Jewish poem) had been found penciled on the wall of a patient's room in an insane asylum after he had been carried to his grave, the general opinion was that this inmate had written the epic in moments of sanity.*

Frederick M. Lehman, "History of the Song, *The Love of God,*" 1948 *(Cyberhymnal.org).*

This unnamed patient, imprisoned both in asylum and mind, dwelt on the steadfast love of God. He penned his prayers on the walls of his prison as an altar of remembrance. He knew that no prison could keep him from the steadfast love of God, but he didn't know that this God of love would transfer his scribbles of faith into a hymn that would encourage future generations. When we place our eternal hope in the steadfast love of God, we too can pen our prayers on the walls of our prisons, breaking them down with the truth which is founded on the everlasting love of our eternal God.

When we walk through fires of adversity or overwhelming floods of pain and sorrow, we must remember God and focus on His attributes which are vaster than the expanding universe. Remembering His works will undergird our courage and faith. Remembering the justice of God allows us to trust Him; He will be our avenger. When there seems to be no hope, we mediate on the power of God which performs miracles and raises the dead to eternal life. We linger long while contemplating the compassion and mercy of God that led Him to give up His sovereign reign in Heaven in order to walk a sin-scarred earth as Savior. Every facet of His nature gives us deeper intimacy with our Savior and widens our trust in the Lover of our soul.

Further Investigation

Song: "I Will Remember You," by Benton Brown

Bible Passage: Psalm 103

Memory verse: I will remember the deeds of the Lord; yes, I will remember your miracles of long ago. I will consider all your works and meditate on all your mighty deeds. Your ways, God, are holy. What god is as great as our God? You are the God who performs miracles; you display your power among the peoples (Psalm 77:11-14 NIV).

Reflective thought: Begin a journal of God's working in your life. Use it as an altar of remembrance. When fears or doubt assail, use it to remember, reflect, meditate, and give thanks to the one who will never leave you.

Prayer:

I will remember you, Oh God. You have been with me since my mother's womb, and I claim your promise to be with me to the end of my days. You have never left me nor forsaken me. When I observe your creation and your works, I remember who you are, and I am assured. Throughout every generation you have met your people with love, compassion, and mercy. You, Oh God, are almighty in power, wisdom, strength, and love. I will trust in you. Amen.

Waiting

In the morning, Lord, you hear my voice; in the morning I lay my requests before you and wait expectantly.

(Psalm 5:3 NIV)

A spirit of restlessness and resistance can never wait, but one who believes he is loved with an everlasting love, and knows that underneath are the everlasting arms, will find strength and peace.

- Elisabeth Elliot

My faith boat was rocking in the storm following my daughter's premature birth. I sat staring into space, unmoving, disbelieving, and being unaware that my two young daughters were observing my unusual behavior. The phone that delivered the current horrific news remained silent now—mocking my denial and disbelief. The doctor's words were reverberating in my brain and refusing to settle into comprehension.

"We have to wait and see," the doctor had explained to me. "Retinopathy of Prematurity progresses for a time, then it will recede. If the blood vessels tug too hard on the retina during the disease progression, the retina could detach. If we get to Stage 3 of the eye disease, we will do laser surgery to prevent a detachment." His voice was tender with an almost imperceptible sigh of emotion. "Surgery is not always successful. If the retina detaches and the surgery is not effective, she will lose her vision."

Tiny fingers of my two-year-old daughter, Chelsey, entwined around mine pulling me back to the present. "Mama. Mama." My mind tried to focus. I attempted a smile, lifted her to my lap and held her close—tightly—baby skin soft and warm against me. I began to rock her gently as if by comforting her I could comfort myself. My eyes closed as I breathed in the scent of baby shampoo. Tears came. I had another baby, a tiny baby that I wanted to rock. A baby in an incubator whom I could not hold. A baby who would wrap her entire hand around my index finger. A baby losing her vision.

"Mama," Chelsey's voice held an adorable firmness, "Mama, Jesus will ho' yo' hand so you wo' fall down." The voice of God was speaking through my two-year-old. I nodded trying to be brave; grieving. She continued, "Like Peter on the boat, Mama. Bemember? Like Peter walking on da watta?"

"Yes," I whispered. I pondered the God who would speak to me out of the mouth of a toddler. "I am like Peter walking on the water," I agreed. *But when he saw the wind, he was afraid, and beginning to sink he cried out, "Lord, save me." Jesus immediately reached out his hand and took hold of him, saying to him, "O you of little faith, why did you doubt?"(Matthew 14:30-31 ESV).*

"Jesus," my heart cried, "my faith is so small. Forgive my doubt of your goodness and your plan. Just as Peter looked at the wind and lost his faith I am looking at my circumstances and drowning. Take my hand. Help me to trust."

Waiting. Born at 25 weeks, eye disease was just one more obstacle in Taylor's battle for life. Each week the eye specialist would examine her. Week after week the disease progressed. "Stage 1, Stage 2A, Stage 2, advanced stage 2, Beginning of Stage 3. "We will just wait a little longer for surgery because laser surgery would cause peripheral blindness," the doctor explained at early stage 3A. Had waiting ever been this hard?

During these weeks and months of waiting, my soul also began to understand spiritual waiting—waiting on God. Leaning hard against Him, entrusting my heart to Him, abiding, persevering. My soul grew. Like fast-growing cells that cause knees to ache on adolescents, it seemed like I had soul cells growing so rapidly that they created pain. I internalized King David's words and made them my own heart's cry. *I wait for the Lord, my soul waits, and in his word I hope; my soul waits for the Lord more than watchman for the morning (Psalm 130: 5-6 ESV).*

God responded. *Wait for the Lord; be strong, and let your heart take courage; wait for the Lord (Psalm 27:14 NASB)!*

God is creative in the ways He gets our attention. As He was teaching me about waiting through His Word, I would see signs every morning on the way to the hospital that declared *Wait*. These were political signs; a man by the name of "Wait" was running for office. But God used those signs to calm me every few blocks. I also found Valentine's Candy hearts with *Wait* printed on them. They made me laugh. God meeting me intimately—reminding me that He was with me every moment of every day.

I prayed, I wept, and I waited. All across the nation people were praying for Taylor and for my family.

We knew six weeks into the eye disease progression that if the disease progressed from a stage 3A to a stage 3 that week, Taylor would need surgery, and she would lose her peripheral vision. The doctor placed a small tool in Taylor's eye to prop the lids open, and she searched Taylor's retina. She looked up from her minute scope. Did I see tears in her eyes? She smiled. "The disease is regressing just in time. Surgery isn't needed." We nearly danced right there in NICU. We were certain that God had totally healed Taylor's retinas.

At fourteen months of age, Taylor began wearing glasses. Eye disease was over, but it had damaged Taylor's retinas leaving them with edges that looked like lattice. Our hopes and prayers for complete healing of Taylor's eyes were not answered as we desired, still, we had much for which to be grateful. We began to realize that Taylor would deal with eye issues all of her life and that waiting on God was also a way of life. We must not just wait through a crisis and then go back to relying on our own strength. We must rest in a perpetual state of waiting on the one who loves us with an everlasting love that we will never fully comprehend.

Time

Our everlasting God is not bound nor pressured by time. He does not rush, nor is He ever late.

> *But do not overlook this one fact, beloved, that with the Lord one day is as a thousand years, and a thousand years as one day. The Lord is not slow to fulfill his promise as some count slowness, but is patient toward you, not wishing that any should perish, but that all should reach repentance (2 Peter 3:8-9 ESV).*

God's timing is perfect as He patiently waits for His will to be accomplished. He is willing to wait for soul growth: acceptance of His will, intimate fellowship with those who abide with Him; strengthened character born from endurance, ripened fruit of the Spirit, or salvation of one who does not yet know Him.

We, on the other hand, tend to be driven by time. It is often our master lashing hard against our backs with a painful whip. It is difficult for us to imagine how little meaning time has in the light of eternity. Time does not rush God. He is willing to wait as long as necessary to accomplish His purpose and will. It is His very patience and compassion that causes the apparent delay in His actions.

Strengthened Character

When we rest in God, waiting for Him to accomplish His purposes during difficult times, He redeems the time. One way He does this is by letting the pain of the difficulties strengthen our character. Strength of character fortifies our hope (Romans 5:3-4). Consequently, our difficulties form us into the image of Christ. When we let God transform us, the fruit of the Spirit becomes more evident in our lives. We walk in the Spirit enjoying intimate fellowship with the God of hope. Love, joy, peace, patience, kindness, goodness, faithfulness, gentleness and self-control become clear evidences that we belong to God. We are transformed into the likeness of the Savior.

The prophet Malachi says that God is like a refiner of silver. *He will sit as a refiner and purifier of silver, and he will purify the sons of Levi and refine them like gold and silver . . . (Malachi 3:3 ESV).* As the silversmith refines the silver in the furnace, so God allows us to be placed in the furnace of affliction. The beauty of our character is often formed in the midst of our greatest trials. A well known short story entitled, "The Silversmith", written by an unknown author, explains the parallels between a silversmith and God. At the end of the story the silversmith says, "When I can see my own image in the silver, the refining process is finished" (Truthbook.com).

When we are refined by the fire that God allows, He can see His likeness in us. The Israelites experienced the Refiner's fire as they endured long periods of waiting for God to intervene while they were captives in Babylon. God spoke to them through the prophet Jeremiah. *"For I know the plans that I have for you," declares the Lord, "plans for welfare and not for calamity to give you a future and a hope"(Jeremiah 29:11 NASB).* God's plan for the Israelite's welfare, however, included seventy years of captivity (Jeremiah 29:10). This was not joyful news to the homesick, grieving Israelites.

God's plan to give them a future and a hope included waiting, abiding in His presence, and living life to its fullest in the midst of chaos and heartache. It included details like building houses, planting gardens, getting married, having children, finding spouses for those children, becoming grandparents, and seeking peace for their captive city. God warned the Israelites against false prophets who would lie to them, telling them what they wanted to hear instead of the true plan of God. God's plan to return them to their homeland would not even begin for seventy years.

Why did God make them wait so long? God knew that this is what it would take to bring His people back to His heart.

> *Then you will call upon me and come and pray to me, and I will hear you. You will seek me and find me, when you seek me with all your heart. I will be found by you, declares the Lord, and I will restore your fortunes and gather you from all the nations and all the places where*

I have driven you, declares the Lord . . . (Jeremiah 29:12-14a ESV).

God was willing to wait for His people to endure enough hardship that they would once again seek Him with their whole heart. When He held their hearts captive, He would release them from the captivity of Babylon.

Seventy years is nothing to God since one thousand years is like a day, but seventy years was a lifetime for the Israelites. A lifetime of learning to call upon the name of God. A lifetime to pray and seek and search for God wholeheartedly. A lifetime of soul growth as they waited for God's timing to return to the Promised Land.

In periods of waiting, it may seem like God delays too long. We wonder why He is slow to respond. We must remember that His timing is perfect. He is the lover of our soul, and He will wait for soul growth. God will wait for His people to love Him wholeheartedly.

Abide

A puppy in obedience school will often run ahead of his master until the leash reins him in. The next moment the puppy lags behind while his owner waits for him to catch up. The goal of obedience school is to teach the puppy to walk alongside its owner. The puppy learns to trust its owner and wait expectantly for direction.

We may be like that puppy in our walk with God. We rush ahead of His plan when we think He delays too long, or we lag behind in obedience when He gives a direction. God desires us to walk with Him in a spirit of prayerfulness, listening for His perfect will and timing. Perhaps God waits until we are truly ready to follow closely—to accept His will—to be yoked to Him as He leads. *"Come to Me, all who are weary and heavy-laden, and I will give you rest. Take my yoke upon you and learn from Me, for I am gentle and humble in heart, and you will find rest for your souls. For my yoke is easy and My burden is light"* (Matthew 11:28-30 NASB).

When we accept God's yoke, we follow closely at the pace He designs while He carries the burden. We learn to walk with our Father like Jesus did—abiding in the soul rest that results in intimate fellowship with Him.

This abiding or soul rest slows us down and creates space for thanksgiving and joy. If we rest in submission, trusting that God does what is best for us, joy in the Lord has room to flourish. Abiding with Jesus promotes joy that is not dependent on one's circumstance. It is a contentment of soul that reposes on Jesus like the Apostle John did at the Passover supper. And like John, we too recognize that we are one whom Jesus loves (John 13:23).

Jesus demonstrated this type of abiding with God in the Garden of Gethsemane. *"My soul is deeply grieved, to the point of death..." (Matthew 26:38 NASB).* Jesus told His disciples about His heartache, and then he sought the Comforter of His soul. *"My Father, if it is possible, let this cup pass from Me; yet not as I will, but as You will" (Matthew 26:39 NASB).* Jesus poured out His heart before God like water, asking for the grace to accept His Father's will, knowing that God would work for the glory of His name.

During times of deep distress we, too, must learn to abide: to seek the Comforter, to trust even when we do not understand, to lean hard into the lover of our soul.

Often waiting times remove us from our busyness. Health issues or job loss can put us into reserve where we feel forgotten or of little use. *Normal* life seems to move past us leaving us stranded and lonely. We may not be able to work, drive, read, or participate in activities that we love. The familiar routines are unattainable.

During these setbacks we have ample time to abide with God. It is so easy to get caught up in the busyness of life—to spend all of our time *doing,* instead of finding time to just *be* in the presence of God. Waiting allows us time to *be* with God without the distractions of every day demands. We have time to contemplate God, to worship, and to meditate with prayer and Scripture reading. When God sets us aside from the flurry of our culture, we can drink deeply of His presence.

If we will stop fretting over all that is not being accomplished during waiting times and learn to *be* in God's presence, we can observe the world around us using all of our senses. We begin to notice the details of God's presence: refracting prisms of rain drops that hang delicately on spring columbine, cloud formations that glide across the azure sky, crickets chirping in the heat of August, gentle breezes soft on skin, or the scent of herbal shampoo wafting from the damp heads of children at bedtime. We recognize the love of God all around us—surrounding us—hemming us in (Psalm 139:5).

Waiting can also allow time to listen to the heartaches of others and to spend concentrated time in prayer for their needs. Getting our mind off of our own troubles relieves us from the temptation of self-pity which is destructive to our well-being.

Our souls have time to learn contentment during waiting episodes. We learn to live in the *now* instead of always seeking tomorrow. We concentrate on the joys of this day instead of wishing them away. So much of our focus can be spent waiting for life to get better, but when that is our outlook—we lose today. Worrying about tomorrow steals the precious moments of this hour.

During surgery for a macular hole, I spent ten days in a face down position. I took time to listen to the stories of my teenagers and their friends, enjoyed the scent of the Blackberry Crème coffee that my husband made in the morning, and viewed the world from a four inch mirror. With my mirror, I was able to focus only on the faces of those who came to visit me. As I watched their expressions, I could see their emotions in their faces: tenderness, concern, and sometimes hilarity as we laughed together at the craziness of my four inch mirror. If all I had focused on were the days ahead when I was well, I would have missed precious moments of life.

Abiding is built-in time with God. Jesus found essential time to get away from the busy crowds to be alone with his Father. During waiting times when we are taken out of our normal schedule, we can spend large blocks of time with God. We find time to abide with our Abba Father, Daddy God.

One of my favorite abiding activities is breathing prayers of Scripture. I read a few verses, pause, meditate, and pray about it. Sometimes they are prayers of confession when the Word convicts, other times I ask for guidance in applying the truths to my own life, and often this precious time leads me to spend time giving God glory and praise. These abiding times become conversations with God over the

Word a few verses at a time. I tell God exactly how I feel; after all, He knows my every thought anyway. I pray through anger and fear, mediate and rest on His promises, and share my joys and hopes with gratitude. These abiding times become precious, intimate times with my Heavenly Father.

Endure and Persevere

Waiting times require endurance. Paul exhorts us to do more than endure; he calls us to rejoice in the hope of the glory of God and the good that He is accomplishing in our lives through our circumstances. Paul explains:

> *Through him we have also obtained access by faith into this grace in which we stand, and we rejoice in hope of the glory of God. More than that, we rejoice in our sufferings, knowing that suffering produces endurance, and endurance produces character, and character produces hope, and hope does not put us to shame, because God's love has been poured into our hearts through the Holy Spirit who has been given to us (Romans 5:2-5 ESV).*

We endure and rejoice for we have bountiful hope in a loving God. Our exultation is based in the one who does all things for His glory and the good of His people.

Noah faced endurance in waiting. It took great endurance and strength to build an ark that has been estimated to be 450 feel long, 75 feet broad, 45 feet high and weighed 14,000 tons. Noah endured the scorn of the people who ridiculed a seeming lunatic who would build an ark on dry ground with no hope of getting it to water. What patience and endurance were required to care for what must have been nearly 17,000 species of animals on a dark, damp, sea-lurching ark for a year while the water first raged, then calmed, and finally rested until it receded? Noah also endured the grief of lost friends and family who refused to listen. Noah's endurance was born from his walk with God and demonstrated his faith and trust despite the circumstances.

Along with endurance goes perseverance—a *never give up* attitude that continues on in faith despite circumstances. Abraham was a man who persevered in his faith against all odds, believing God would keep

His promise and give Abraham a son. Abraham was one hundred years old when Isaac was born. Abraham had already demonstrated years of perseverance through the long drought of waiting. Against all odds, Abraham had hope.

> *Without weakening in his faith, he faced the fact that his body was as good as dead—since he was about a hundred years old—and that Sarah's womb was also dead. Yet he did not waver through unbelief regarding the promise of God, but was strengthened in his faith and gave glory to God, being fully persuaded that God had power to do what he had promised. This is why "it was credited to him as righteousness" (Romans 4:19-22 NIV).*

Abraham persevered in the faith despite the circumstances that made it seem that God's promise could not be fulfilled. Abraham remembered that God had the power to do what He had promised, and Abraham gave God glory.

Waiting for Eternity

On the day that Jesus returns or calls us home, our sorrows will end. Perhaps Job said it best. *All the days of my struggle I will wait until my change comes. You will call, and I will answer You; You will long for the work of Your hands (Job 14:14b-15 NASB).* Our hearts will sing in praise on the day that we meet Jesus face to face.

Until that day, we wait for God to accomplish His purpose in our life here on earth. We wait for soul growth and for lessons in contentment to take root. We rest in His sovereignty, for He is the God of time. Rushing, hurrying and worrying will not make answers come any sooner. Instead, we must be content with the joys of the day and the pleasures of the hour. We love today, laugh today, sing today, and praise today while we wait. We do not know what tomorrow brings (James 4:14), but whatever it is—God is already there.

Further Investigation

Song: "Everlasting God," by Chris Tomlin

Memory Verse: *Though youths grow weary and tired, and vigorous young men stumble badly, yet those who wait for the Lord will gain new strength; they will mount up with wings like eagles, they will run and not get tired, they will walk and not become weary (Isaiah 40:31 NASB).*

Bible Passage: Psalm 40

Reflective question: How might waiting times encourage soul growth?

Prayer:

I will wait for you, Oh God, to accomplish your will and purpose in my life. Help me to persevere in faith by abiding in you even when the waiting seems long. I will trust your timing, for time is boundless and eternal with you. I will abide near your heart sheltered under your wings. Amen.

Ever-Present Help

God is our refuge and strength, an ever-present help in trouble.

(Psalm 46:1 NIV)

Few delights can equal the mere presence of one
whom we trust utterly. –George MacDonald

Grief ambushed Ardy. Until now she had been rejoicing that Carlton, her dear husband, was with the Lord. At the funeral, Ardy was one of few who didn't weep. Instead, her face had radiated the joys she shared with her loved one now gone from here but home with the Lord. For him there was no more sorrow, no more pain, no more tears.

Now, though, as she subconsciously strained to hear Carlton's voice, all that responded was the hum of the furnace. Despair raised its head from its sleeping position and overwhelmed the widow with tidal sorrow. She rocked slightly, her gray head bent, and through tears she inspected her hands that would no longer be held by his.

Trying to fill the empty time that loomed before her, Ardy aimlessly browsed through Carlton's books. One in particular caught her eye. She chuckled as she lifted it off the shelf and brushed dust off its cover. Carlton, or Cot as he was affectionately called because his hair was as white as cotton, had given her this book fifty years ago. She had never read it, but she clearly remembered the incident.

The memory of the time during WWII was still vivid in her mind. One of their last times together before Cot went to war, they had drifted into the campus bookstore while walking around Moody Bible Institute.

"Look how many copies of that book they have ordered," Ardy had pointed to a stack of commentaries on *The Song of Solomon*. "Sure must be popular!" It had been a casual comment to break the awkward silence between them that was filled with all the things of which they were afraid to speak.

The next day Cot gave her a copy of the book just before he left for the war. Ardy could still remember the heat of the blush that crept up her neck to her cheeks. What must he think of her? Did he think that by calling attention to the book, she was making insinuations about what she had hoped for in their relationship? *The Song of Solomon* was a poetic romance dialoguing intimate feelings between newlyweds. After Cot left, she had crammed the book into a stuffed bookshelf—embarrassed. By the time the war was over and they were married, the long forgotten book remained unread and abandoned.

Fifty years had passed since the day Cot gave Ardy the book—fifty years of happiness together. Ardy held the now priceless book in her hand. No flush of embarrassment swept over her this time. Instead a sweet joy began to ebb its way back into her soul.

As she opened the cover for the first time, her eyes filled with tears. On the inside cover was a personal message written by her husband while he was a young soldier possibly facing death. It was a message to her—a message of encouragement in case he never came back to continue the romance they had started before the war. She had never read the message because she had never opened the book.

Had God hidden and saved this message for fifty years for this time when despair had nearly taken root in the fertile soil of her grief? It was as if Cot were reaching down from Heaven with one final unexpected message and charge to her. Psalm 37:5 was neatly printed in ink that was now faded. *Commit thy way unto the Lord; trust also in Him; and he shall bring it to pass" (KJV).* Cot had written a poem that followed the

Scripture. The encouragement from both God and Carlton read:

Eternal Day

No doubt shall ever shade my brow

Nor sad mistrust;

Be this my solemn, earnest vow;

Trust him, I must.

What'er befalls, change or decay;

He'll walk with me, and mark the way,

And guide me to Eternal Day;

Be true, he must.

Carlton Kloster

Floodgates opened, and long pent-up tears let loose to stream down the age-worn lines in Ardy's face. How God must love her to reveal this precious message after fifty years—at the exact time it would be most meaningful to her after Cot's death! Cot's reminder that God was with them always, in life or in death, resonated in Ardy's soul. Trust displaced despair. Joy, in the midst of grief, returned as she looked forward to the *Eternal Day* Cot had described in his poem.

Ardy is my mother-in-law. She is a sweet woman of faith whose trust in God seems divinely unwavering. During her dark days of near depression after Cot died, she abided with Jesus continually. We family members would visit her and find her worship music blaring as she sat in her rocker with her eyes closed. Though she was glad to see us, she would drift back into worship, even in the midst of conversation. Periodically, she would be startled as if she had forgotten we were there. She was lost in the presence of her Savior.

The day I found her with the precious book that contained the message from my father-in-law; joy seemed to radiate from her face. She recognized the love of her Abba Father in His ever-present help. God had gone before her for fifty years to preserve a message for the time Cot was called home to glory—not on the battlefield of WWII in Germany, but after a long life fully lived. God's ever-present help and love hemmed Mom in behind and before (Psalm 139).

God is with Us

God is in our past, our present, and our future. He knows when we sit, when we lie down to sleep, and when we rise. Our thoughts are discerned by Him because He is ever near—living inside the souls of his children. Closer than our breath, He knows us better than we know ourselves. Out of dust we are created, and out of dust He makes glorious life. Our path is searched by Him, and He is intimately acquainted with all of our ways. When no one else is with us, God is. We are never alone for He indwells those who make Him Lord of their life.

There is nowhere we can go that God is not there. Even if we wanted to flee from Him, we could not. If we ascend to Heaven, He is there! If we dive to the uttermost parts of the sea, even there His hand leads us and holds us tight. Darkness and light are not different to Him; therefore no darkness of night or soul can keep us from Him. He is our Maker, the One who knit us in our mother's womb, and He will never leave us nor forsake His own (Psalm 139).

There are times in life when no one understands our pain. We cannot explain it, and even if someone has gone through a similar circumstance, they will not feel or respond exactly like us. But God knows. Our Maker knows our every thought and emotion. His ever-present help beckons us to abide—to rest in Him—to *be* in His presence. God is intimate with the upright (Proverbs 3:32), and He never slumbers nor sleeps (Psalm 121:3). We can pour out our hearts to the one who resides in our soul. Because of God's ever-present help, when we are near despair we can echo the words of Psalm 94:17-19. *If the Lord had not been my help, my soul would soon have lived in the land of silence. When I thought, "My foot slips," your steadfast love, O Lord, held me up. When the cares of my heart are many, your consolations cheer my soul"* (Psalm 94:17-19 ESV).

From hospital nurseries to the seemingly abandoned in nursing home beds, God is there. God loves us just as He did the house of Jacob to whom He declared: *Listen to me, O house of Jacob, all the remnant of the house of Israel, who have been borne by me from before your birth, carried from the womb; even to your old age I am he, and to gray hairs I will carry you. I have made, and I will bear; I will carry and will save (Isaiah 46:3-4 ESV).*

God carries us when we feel we can no longer take another step. I still remember how it felt to be carried by my father when I was just a little girl. I remember my weariness, and how good it felt not to have to walk any further. Dad would lift me easily, and I would lay my head on his shoulder—body draping long and loose—barely even bothering to hang on, for I knew Dad would not let me fall. I felt safe, protected and loved. God says He carries us like that. Our Abba Father carries us when we are too weary to take another step.

Even when we aren't aware of His presence, God carries us. He is not bound by time, space, or our idea of who He is. There are times when we just don't *feel* God with us. During those times, it is essential to listen and watch for God—to ask Him to reveal himself to us. When we quiet our soul, we find Him in Scripture, nature, music, literature, and in the love of His people. If we ask God to reveal himself to us, we will see Him everywhere.

When I was on bed rest for months during a difficult pregnancy, I could hear life going on without me in the rest of the house—the giggles of children, the smell of chicken frying, the rustle of homework papers. Loneliness caused my heart to ache. I called out to God, "Lord, I don't even feel as if you are here with me." Longing to feel God's presence and hear His voice, I opened the Word of God and found the following verses.

Nevertheless, I am continually with you; you hold my right hand. You guide me with your counsel, and afterward you will receive me to glory. Whom have I in Heaven but you? And there is nothing on earth that I desire besides you. My flesh and my heart may fail, but God is the strength of my heart and my portion forever" (Psalm 73:23-26 ESV).

No matter how I felt, God assured me that He was continually with me. He was holding my hand, guiding me, and helping me turn to the very Scriptures my soul needed at the moment.

My heart responded to God with another verse in that chapter. *But*

for me it is good to be near God; I have made the Lord God my refuge...
(Psalm 73: 28a ESV).

Despite my lonely feelings, God was with me. I could talk to Him at any moment of the day or night. I began to dwell on thanks—for the laughter of the children, for the chicken frying in the kitchen, and for the love of my husband who works all day and comes home to care for his family. God was all around me; I just needed to open my eyes to see Him.

God is with us in every circumstance of our life. He is our refuge and strength in each difficulty. Though life is almost unbearably hard at times, we have a shelter—and that shelter is God. We run to Him and find cover under the shelter of His wings. He is a very present help in troubled times.

We do not need to fear, for our Sovereign God is in control. Everything passes through His hands. If we seek Him, He will comfort and guide us through all of life. Psalm 46:1-3 declares: *God is our refuge and strength, a very present help in trouble. Therefore we will not fear though the earth gives way, though the mountains be moved into the heart of the sea, though its waters roar and foam, though the mountains tremble at its swelling (ESV).* When we place our faith in the God who never leaves our side, fear will flee.

How wonderful to know that the Lord of hosts, the Creator of this universe, the God of all—is with each of us! Nothing escapes His notice. *For the eyes of the Lord run to and fro throughout the whole earth, to give strong support to those whose heart is blameless toward him (2 Chronicles 16:9 ESV).* He is always watching just as a parent guards a child. He is aware and alert to danger and ready to come to our aid when we call on His name. He hears the sound of our weeping and listens to our pleas (Psalm 6:8-*9).* The Apostle Paul joyfully proclaimed, *If God is for us, who can be against us (Romans 8: 31b ESV)?*

Does this mean that everything will work out as we hope? God's ways are higher than ours. When we do not understand His ways, we must trust His heart.

God Goes Before Us

Just as God went before my mother-in-law to prepare what she needed in the future, He goes before each of us. He is not bound by time. His foreknowledge extends into eternity. Trusting God with our future brings peace.

Apart from God, we would have every reason to dread the future, for we would have no respite or resting place. Our hearts would tremble and our souls languish. Our lives would hang in doubt, and we would live in dread night and day with no assurance for our life (Deuteronomy 28:65-66). For those who follow Christ; however, we have no reason to live a life of dread. The prophet Isaiah quoted God:

> *"You are not to say, 'It is a conspiracy!' in regard to all that this people call a conspiracy, and you are not to fear what they fear or be in dread of it. It is the Lord of hosts whom you should regard as holy. And He shall be your fear, and He shall be your dread. Then He shall become a sanctuary . . ."(Isaiah 8:12-14a NASB).*

When we rest in the assurance that God goes ahead of us, we can face the future with strength and courage. The Israelites demonstrated how fear of the future reflects a lack of faith. By covenant God had given the Israelites the Promised Land. Yet when the spies returned with a report of the strength and fortification of the people that they were to overtake, the Israelites let fear rule their hearts and decisions. They refused to go into the land which the spies had declared was flowing with milk and honey; instead, they wandered in the wilderness for forty years that could have been lived in the Promised Land.

The Book of Deuteronomy records the fears of the Israelites. *"The people are greater and taller than we. The cities are great and fortified up to Heaven. And besides, we have seen the sons of the Anakim there"* (Deuteronomy 1:28b ESV).

Moses responded:

> *"Do not be in dread or afraid of them. The Lord your*

> *God who goes before you will himself fight for you, just as he did for you in Egypt before your eyes, and in the wilderness, where you have seen how the Lord your God carried you, as a man carries his son, all the way that you went until you came to this place"* (Deut. 1: 29-31 ESV).

In Moses' response we see God as his Abba Father, Daddy God. God carried the Israelites through the wilderness as a father carries a son. He provided manna for them, led them by pillar and fire, and even made their shoes so that they did not wear out or cause their feet to swell.

After wandering in the desert for forty years, the Israelites finally trusted God with their future. After Moses died, the Israelites entered the Promised Land under Joshua's leadership. God promised Joshua and the Israelites: *Just as I was with Moses, so I will be with you. I will not leave you or forsake you (Joshua 1:5b ESV).*

Be Strong and Courageous

As the Israelites entered the Promised Land, God charged them to be strong and courageous. Courage would dispel the fear that had caused them to wander in the wilderness for forty years. *Have I not commanded you? Be strong and courageous. Do not be frightened, and do not be dismayed, for the Lord your God is with you wherever you go (Joshua 1:9 ESV).*

Faith and fear are opposing attributes. When we have fear, our faith is weak. When our faith is strong, fear will flee. This leaves courage to face the future, because we trust that God is by our side. When we walk closely with God, following His ways and meditating on His Word, we know our future is secure. Whatever God calls us to do will be successful. He will prosper the work He has given to us, and success in our life's purpose will be certain.

Courage enables us to accomplish the task that God sets before us; it doesn't guarantee that life will be easy. Courage is not fearlessness; it is God-given ability to vanquish fear with faith. Many missionaries have died for the sake of Christ after courageously following Him to the mission field. Darlene Rose and Elisabeth Elliot are examples of women who lost their husbands in the warfare of mission fields only to return to the very land that robbed them of their loved ones.

Such lives attest to the truth that there is no God-forsaken place. Having the courage to return to the land of the very enemies that killed their husbands led many people to place their trust in Christ. Elisabeth Elliot's unconditional love for the Auca people transformed the tribe as they learned to follow Jesus. In her book, *Evidence Not Seen,* Darlene Rose chronicled the names of fifteen missionary martyrs with whom she had worked in Japanese prisoner of war camps or in the jungles of Borneo. Referring to these martyrs, Rose explained her return to New Guinea like this: "Out of the past and from the distant shore, I hear them calling, 'Run, Darlene, run! Run with perseverance the race that is set before you. It is worth it all!'" (Rose).

This seemingly superhuman courage and resolve for the kingdom can drive each of our lives, for each of us has the same God as Elliot and Rose. Let us put on the armor of God and courageously face whatever comes. God is with us in the battle.

We need courage and strength to face every day; they are not just a requirement for martyrdom. God's ever-present help bolsters our courage. On the morning of my first chemotherapy session, I woke with the dread of the day. I poured out my heart before the Lord. "Father, I wanted to wake up and find that this was all a bad dream. This can't be real. I don't want to have chemo. I don't want to be sick. I don't like this Lord." I was consumed with self-pity as my thoughts turned down dark recesses of the mind.

Suddenly and unexplainably, the radio popped on. It was neither the typical time that the alarm was set nor the typical local classical station by which we generally were wakened. A voice came across the air waves from a Christian station, "It doesn't matter what you think. It matters what God thinks. And this is what God thinks. You are more than conquerors through Jesus Christ your Lord!"

I laughed out loud. "Thank you, God. You are so very good. Thank you for meeting me right where I am. Yes, through you and your strength and grace I can conquer anything—cancer, chemo, life or death."

This encounter was divine intervention and the ever-present help of God. He is with us every moment of every day, and He gives us the courage to fight the battles that come our way. *In all these things we are more than conquerors through him who loved us (Romans 8:37 ESV).*

God Fights for Us

God calls us to courage in the midst of life's battles, but He also promises to fight for us if we belong to Him. After the Promised Land was conquered and the Israelites had rest on all sides, Joshua, who was now well advanced in years, reminded the Israelites that God had fought for them in the battle. *And you have seen all that the Lord your God has done to all these nations for your sake, for it is the Lord your God who has fought for you (Joshua 23:3 ESV).* Then Joshua charged the Israelites to be very strong and to follow the ways of God, clinging to God always just as they had clung to Him in the midst of the battle. Joshua reminded them to *be very careful, therefore, to love the Lord your God (Joshua 23: 11 ESV).*

If we love God and walk with Him closely, He will fight for us. If we turn away from God and fight our battles in our own strength, failure is sure to follow.

Later in the history of the Israelites, enemies marched against Israel under the reign of King Jehoshaphat. The king reminded His people how God had fought for them when they conquered the Promised Land. Jehoshaphat was afraid, but in his fear he sought the Lord. King Jehoshaphat prayed:

> *O Lord, God of our fathers, are you not God in Heaven? You rule over all the kingdoms of the nations. In your hand are power and might, so that none is able to withstand you. . . . If disaster comes upon us, the sword, judgment, or pestilence, or famine, we will stand before this house and before you—for your name is in this house—and cry out to you in our affliction, and you will hear and save. . . . For we are powerless against this great horde that is coming against us. We do not know what to do, but our eyes are on you (2 Chronicles 20: 6, 9,& 12b ESV).*

Under King Jehoshaphat, the Israelites stood before God with their wives and children, and God spoke to them through the prophet Jahaziel: *Do not be afraid and do not be dismayed at this great horde, for the battle is not yours but God's. . . . Do not be afraid and do not be dismayed. Tomorrow go out against them, and the Lord will be with you (2 Chronicles 20: 15b & 17 ESV).*

The enemies of King Jehoshaphat's Israelite army turned against each other and destroyed one other. Israel never even engaged in battle. The Israelites took the spoils from the battleground, and they named the valley that had caused so much fear and weeping *The Valley of Beracah* or The Valley of Blessing. *So the realm of Jehoshaphat was quiet, for his God gave him rest all around (2 Chronicles 20: 30 ESV).*

God is with us in every battle we face if we cling to Him. He fights for us. When we don't know what to do, we keep our eyes on Him. When we are powerless, we seek God for wisdom and help. The battles of life are not ours; they are God's. He is in control of all things. He is the God of Heaven and earth, and like King Jehoshaphat, we put our trust in Him. We meditate on all that we know to be true about God to strengthen our resolve and courage. We fight fear with faith, trusting God no matter what the circumstance, for He is with us. He will never leave us or forsake us. He is an ever-present help in trouble.

Further Investigation

Song: "God with Us," by Mercy Me

Bible Passage: Psalm 139

Memory verse: God is our refuge and strength, an ever-present help in trouble *(Psalm 46:1 NASB).*

Reflective activity: Journal about times you have strongly felt God's presence. How did He make himself known to you?

Prayer:

Ever-present God,

    Please reveal yourself to me. Help me to know that you are with me. Wrap your arms around me and remind me that you will never leave me or forsake me. Teach me to cling to you, to seek you at all times, to trust you with all of my heart. Replace my fears with faith, and strengthen me with the courage that comes from you, so that I can face whatever comes. You are God. I trust that you are in control of the battles of my life, that you fight for me, and that you are with me wherever I go. You hem me in before and behind with your love. Strengthen me according to your Word. Amen.

Choice and a Fallen World

"You may surely eat of every tree of the garden, but of the tree of the knowledge of good and evil you shall not eat, for in the day that you eat of it you shall surely die."

(Genesis 2:16b-17 ESV)

When you and I hurt deeply, what we really need is not an explanation from God but a revelation of God. We need to see how great God is; we need to recover our lost perspective on life. Things get out of proportion when we are suffering, and it takes a vision of something bigger than ourselves to get life's dimensions adjusted again.

-Warren W. Wiersbe

    Tranquility and refuge beckon from behind the garden gate. Come rest with me among lush green hues of scented bush, towering tree and swaying grass. Keep time with garden rhythms: creak of branch, tap of woodpecker, and the whisper of purple violets gentle and low in the breeze. Gaze at the joy of zinnia dances brilliant in costume and showy in height. Breathe deeply of roses climbing wildly over arches like children on playgrounds. Hum gently to the lilting songs of flashing birds or a singing brook over boulders. Keep joyful rhythm with the buzz of bees, chirp of crickets, and chatter of squirrels. Inhale deeply the earthy smells of life and the fragrant gifts of Heaven. Gardens beckon to our soul in their wild beauty. Lay your weary bones and souls on grassy fields. Gaze with imagination at azure skies and white clouds. Abide with your Maker in the peace of the garden.

Throughout time, writers and lyricists have written about the soul healing of gardens. This is no surprise when we remember that life on earth started in a garden—paradise. All other gardens are shadows of the radiance and harmony of paradise. Legends of Utopia echo back to Eden and forward to Heaven.

Nature is a channel of God's peace and grace. King David detailed his intimate walks with God in nature. *The Lord is my shepherd; I shall not want. He makes me lie down in green pastures. He leads me beside still waters. He restores my soul (Psalm 23:1-3a ESV).*

The soul restoration to which David referred has long been a byproduct of nature walks with God. Jesus found strength, comfort, and guidance from His Father in the gardens of the world: mountain tops, the wilderness, secluded places during early morning dawn, and during his last hours on earth in The Garden of Gethsemane.

What secret does nature hold to provide healing and restoration? The garden is the original place where God walked intimately with His children. All that God created in the Garden of Eden was good and reflected the very nature of God's own goodness. When God breathed into the nostrils of Adam, he became a living soul designed to enjoy the splendor of the garden in the presence of God.

So what went wrong? Why was paradise barred? Why is life so painful now? Surely, the most heart-wrenching theological question is, "How can a good God allow so much pain, sorrow, and suffering?"

Suffering is a result of evil, and evil thrives because God allows free will. God designed humans to have choice. He designed relationships to be dependent upon love rather than obligation or force of will. Obligation and force rob relationships of joy and meaning. God wants what we want, relationships where love and desire for intimacy are reciprocal. He wants our hearts, not simply outward obedience. Our loving Father outlines holiness, explains consequences of sin, and allows each of us to decide if we will walk intimately with Him.

Human choice began in the Garden of Eden where God planted the tree of the knowledge of good and evil. This was the only tree from which Adam and Eve were not allowed to eat. *"You may surely eat of every tree of the garden, but of the tree of the knowledge of good and evil you shall not eat, for in the day that you eat of it you shall surely die" (Genesis 2:16b ESV).* Adam and Eve had a choice. They could walk intimately with their Father in the garden, resting in His love and trusting that He knew what was best for them, or they could choose their own way and suffer the consequences of broken fellowship with their Creator.

It is the same choice we have today. Over and over in Scripture God links our love for Him with obedience. If we truly love Him with all of our heart, we will obey Him out of a deep reverence and trust in an all loving Father who does what is best for us. Distrust leads to disobedience, and disobedience reflects a lack of love. Love is a choice that is demonstrated as an action.

> *Love is patient and kind; love does not envy or boast; it is not arrogant or rude. It does not insist on its own way; it is not irritable or resentful; it does not rejoice at wrongdoing, but rejoices with the truth. Love bears all things, believes all things, hopes all things, endures all things. Love never ends (1 Corinthians 13: 4-8a ESV).*

Love guards our hearts from which the wellsprings of life flow.

As soon as Adam and Eve acted upon their distrust in God, which demonstrated a lack of love, their intimate fellowship with Him in the garden was broken. Shame was immediate and death was inevitable. Adam and Eve hid from God, their Creator, and the one who created all things good. They hid from the lover of their souls. How much sorrow and shame must have overwhelmed them when their eyes were open to evil! Their very act of disobedience had ushered in their understanding of evil from which they had been protected. The horrors of consequence were just beginning to dawn.

How God's words must have haunted them even as they haunt us today when our sin creates devastation! *"What is this that you have done?" (Genesis 3:13 ESV).* Can you hear the sorrow in God's voice? God began to list the consequences of their distrust and disobedience:

enmity, pain, suffering, subjection to the power of others, curse, toil, banishment, death, and decay. Thorn and thistles of ground would require the sweat of the body to eradicate; soul healing would require the death of the Savior.

In mercy, God would no longer let Adam and Eve live in paradise. This protected them from eating of the Tree of Life that would grant them immortality in a fallen world of suffering. Death became the exit to this fallen world, and Jesus would conquer death allowing eternal life with God in Heaven where there was no more sin, sorrow, suffering, or tears.

Adam and Eve's shame, manifested in their sudden awareness of their nakedness, God covered with animal skins. These sacrificial skins symbolized the required shedding of blood for the remission of sin. They were a foreshadowing of Christ's sacrifice on the cross (Hebrews 9:22). The consequence of sin is death, but God's mercy is victorious over death. Jesus would take the punishment of sin upon himself so that intimate fellowship with His children would be restored. Mercy triumphs over judgment (James 2:13).

Until Christ's return, evil will try to dominate our world. The long, hard road of suffering on earth had begun. Jealousy and rivalry resulted in murder when Adam and Eve's firstborn son, Cain, killed his brother, Abel. Grief and feelings of guilt must have overwhelmed Adam and Eve. What had they begun on the day that they first distrusted God? When God told them that they would surely die if they ate of the tree of the knowledge of good and evil, they had not believed Him. Death had taken their beloved son at the hand of the same evil they had failed to reject.

Cain had been warned of the consequences of sin just as his parents had been. *...sin is crouching at the door. Its desire is for you, but you must rule over it (Genesis 4:7b ESV).* Cain chose sin—just as when we choose sin today. *For all have sinned and fall short of the glory of God (Romans 3:23 NASB).* Each of us battles the evil in our soul, that was first introduced in Eden. The Apostle Paul explained the battle against evil that rages in each of our souls. *For I do not understand my own actions. For I do not do what I want, but I do the very thing I hate (Romans 7:15 ESV).*

Thankfully, we have the Holy Spirit who allows us the victory over evil when we abide with our Maker. The Apostle Paul rejoiced in this hope:

> *So I find it to be a law that when I want to do right, evil lies close at hand. For I delight in the law of God, in my inner being, but I see in my members another law waging war against the law of my mind and making me captive to the law of sin that dwells in my members. Wretched man that I am! Who will deliver me from this body of death? Thanks be to God through Jesus Christ our Lord (Romans 7:21-25a ESV)!*

All of creation was subjected to futility once evil entered the world (Romans 8:20). Living in a fallen world is the root cause of the suffering on earth. Even natural disasters that result in horrific loss of life are a result of living in a world gone awry. The battle of good and evil continues on earth and in the spiritual realm. Satan roams the earth like a roaring lion seeking whom he may devour (1 Peter 5:8). He stands before God day and night accusing us of the very sins of which we are guilty (Revelations 12:10). Evil will not be completely eradicated until Christ returns; therefore, the battle with evil continues in the world and in our souls.

Praise God that it won't always be this way! Creation waits with eager longing for Christ's return. At that time creation will be set free from its bondage of corruption and will be restored to its former glory. There will be a new Heaven and a new earth. Everything that has been skewed and twisted by evil will be made glorious. In the meantime, those of us who have the first fruits of the Spirit groan inwardly as we eagerly await the redemption of our bodies. Our new bodies will no longer ache with the suffering of disease and death or the consequences of evil. In these thoughts we place our hope, and this hope will not disappoint us.

God's Heart

Where is God in this tragic fallen world? He is among us. He is the core of all existence and the one who holds all things together.

God wrapped himself in flesh and took on human form. His

redemptive plan brought Him to the earth He created, the earth that is now ravaged by sin and sorrow. He walked the path of pain that each of us walks. Cold hearts rejected Him even before His birth; there was no room for Him to be born in the busy inns of Bethlehem. Delivered into a cold, hostile world as an outcast, His first crib was a dirty feed trough for animals. No princely robes for the King of Kings; there were only swaddling cloths to warm Him. His birth created immediate chaos. King Herod, feeling threatened, slaughtered all baby boys under the age of two in Bethlehem and the surrounding region. God was born into a grieving, heart-broken world.

The Book of Matthew records this time as the fulfillment of Jeremiah's prophecy. *"A voice was heard in Ramah, weeping and loud lamentation, Rachel weeping for her children; she refused to be comforted, because they are no more." (Matthew 2:18 ESV).* Further dark prophecies surrounded Jesus' birth. Simeon, whom the Holy Spirit was upon, proclaimed to Jesus' mother, Mary: *"Behold, this child is appointed for the fall and rising of many in Israel, and for a sign that is opposed (and a sword will pierce through your own soul also), so that thoughts from many hearts may be revealed." (Luke 2:34-35ESV).*

As an adult, Jesus walked with those who were downtrodden, sorrowful, and scorned. He was near to those in need of salvation and comfort, because seeking the lost is the very heart of God. The Pharisees and scribes scoffed at one who would minster to blatant offenders of the laws of God. *"This man receives sinners and eats with them." (Luke 15:1 ESV).* Yet they did not recognize the evil in their own heart motives that were every bit as vile as those they judged as unworthy.

Jesus explained His heart's desire for the lost in the parable of the prodigal son. God waits with hopeful expectation for the repentant heart to return home. Broken, the prodigal son cried, *"Father, I have sinned against Heaven and before you. I am no longer worthy to be called your son." (Luke 15:21ESV).* And our God of all mercy responds as the father of the prodigal responded. *"Bring quickly the best robe, and put it on him, and put a ring on his hand, and shoes on his feet. And bring the fattened calf and kill it, and let us eat and celebrate. For this my son was dead, and is alive again; he was lost, and is found." And they began to celebrate (Luke 15:22-24 ESV).*

God dwelt among us, and then He took our sins and our sorrows upon himself. Nailed to a tree, He bore our shame so we could be reconciled to Him. Our God of love and compassion joined in our suffering and sorrow. He was a man of sorrows and acquainted with grief (Isaiah 53:3). He understands our pain.

Even in the face of evil, God's heart is one of love for His children. He longs for His children to come to Him. God's heart of longing, love, and compassion is expressed in the Book of Matthew. *O Jerusalem, Jerusalem, the city that kills the prophets and stones those who are sent to it! How often would I have gathered your children together as a hen gathers her brood under her wings, and you would not (Matthew 23:37 ESV)!*

God waits and watches for the day when we will finally turn to Him. He releases us to our own choices like the father of the prodigal released his son, but He also longingly awaits our return, just as the father of the prodigal expectantly waited. *But while he was still a long way off, his father saw him and felt compassion, and ran and embraced him and kissed him (Luke 15:20b ESV).*

George MacDonald explained it like this:

> *Instead of crushing the power of evil by divine force; instead of compelling justice and destroying the wicked; instead of making peace on the earth by the rule of a perfect prince; instead of gathering the children of Jerusalem under His wings whether they would or not, and saving them from the horrors that anguished His prophetic soul—He let evil work its will while it lived . . .To love righteousness is to make it grow, not to avenge it. . . .*

And when we do turn to God, saved by grace through faith in Christ, He sends the Holy Spirit to guide and comfort us. The Holy Spirit of God will never leave us nor forsake us; He is with us every moment of every day. God is with us in our pain, and He encourages us to not lose heart while living in this fallen world.

Do not Lose Heart

The Apostle Paul wrote about pain and suffering on earth with an eternal perspective. *We are afflicted in every way, but not crushed; perplexed, but not driven to despair; persecuted, but not forsaken; struck down, but not destroyed;. . . (2 Corinthians 4:8 ESV)*. Even in our darkest hours, we have the hope of God in our hearts:

> *So we do not lose heart. Though our outer self is wasting away, our inner self is being renewed day by day. For this light momentary affliction is preparing for us an eternal weight of glory beyond all comparison, as we look not to the things that are seen but to the things that are unseen. For the things that are seen are transient, but the things that are unseen are eternal (2 Corinthians 416-18 ESV).*

What then do we do with our sorrows while we walk this earth? We cast them upon Jesus because He cares for us (I Peter 5:7). We resist the urge to despair and stand firm in our faith, knowing that many on earth have suffered similar experiences in this world of grief. We support each other with prayer, good deeds, and words of encouragement. We rest in the hope of restoration. The Apostle Paul encourages us in our suffering: *And after you have suffered a little while, the God of all grace, who has called you to his eternal glory in Christ, will himself restore, confirm, strengthen, and establish you (1 Peter 5: 10 ESV).*

This earthly life and this earthly body are temporary. In God's perspective one thousand years is the same as a day (2 Peter 3:8), so in God's eyes, our life on earth is very short—a pinpoint of time on a vast eternal scale. The Apostle Peter had this perspective. *All flesh is like grass and all its glory like the flower of grass. The grass withers, and the flower falls, but the word of the Lord remains forever (1 Peter 1:24-25 ESV).* With his death imminent, Peter reminded followers of Christ that *we are waiting for new Heavens and a new earth in which righteousness dwells (2 Peter 3:13 ESV).*

And this new Heaven and earth will be *an inheritance that is imperishable, undefiled, and unfading, kept in Heaven for you. . . (1 Peter 1:4 ESV).* Focusing on our future eternal inheritance inspires joy and peace in the midst of pain. *In this you rejoice, though now for a little while, if necessary, you have been grieved by various trials (1 Peter 1:6 ESV).*

In the meantime, God transforms the pain of His children into soul growth and glory. In our suffering we cling to the one who is our only hope in a dark world. In this abiding, our love for God allows us to walk in love and obedience with our Maker—desiring His will for our lives. The Apostle Peter encouraged: *Since therefore Christ suffered in the flesh, arm yourselves with the same way of thinking, for whoever has suffered in the flesh has ceased from sin, so as to live for the rest of the time in the flesh no longer for human passions but for the will of God (1 Peter 4:1-2 ESV).*

Finally, the Apostle Peter reminds us that all suffering passes through the hands of God. Though evil exists in our fallen world, God is still sovereign, and He allows our pain for His eternal purposes. Peter encourages us to trust God in our pain. *Therefore, those also who suffer according to the will of God shall entrust their souls to a faithful Creator in doing what is right (1 Peter 4:19 NASB).* We can entrust even our suffering to God who always does what is right.

Praise Anyway

The prophet Habakkuk had moments of near despair living in a fallen world. His heart cried out to God, spilling out like water before the Almighty. Unashamed and unafraid to speak his heart, Habakkuk cried to God:

> *O Lord, how long shall I cry for help, and you will not hear? Or cry to you "Violence!" and you will not save? Why do you make me see iniquity, and why do you idly look at wrong? Destruction and violence are before me; strife and contention arise. So the law is paralyzed, and justice never goes forth. For the wicked surround the righteous; so justice goes forth perverted (Habakkuk 1:2-4 ESV).*

Like Habakkuk, when our heart is breaking, we can tell our sorrows and complaints to the God who already knows our words before they are on our tongue (Psalm 139:4). We need not be ashamed of our emotions. Jesus wept at the ravages of sin on earth, why wouldn't we?

And our faithful God will answer us just as He answered Habakkuk. *Look among the nations, and see; wonder and be astounded. For I am doing a work in your days that you would not believe if told (Habakkuk 1:5 ESV).* These could be God's words to us: watch, wait, and see what I am doing. Nothing God does is an accident or a mistake. Everything passes through the hands of God.

Habakkuk even questioned God. *You who are of purer eyes than to see evil and cannot look at wrong, why do you idly look at traitors and remain silent when the wicked swallows up the man more righteous than he (Habakkuk 1:13 ESV)?* Do not our own hearts echo these thoughts at times? Why, God? Why do you allow this?

When our hearts are troubled, we must expectantly wait to hear from God, like Habakkuk did. *I will take my stand at my watchpost and station myself on the tower, and look out to see what he will say to me, and what I will answer concerning my complaint (Habakkuk 2:1 ESV).* Was Habakkuk bold in his questions to God? Certainly! Yet, Habakkuk had absolute confidence in God. God assured Habakkuk that justice would prevail and that the righteous must live by faith, clinging to God's promises even when we do not understand His ways.

After Habakkuk's long discourse with God, his soul quieted and rejoiced in the one who knew better than he. Habakkuk vowed to trust God even in the midst of a fallen world—even in the heart of pain and sorrow. Our hearts would do well to echo his prayer.

> *Though the fig tree should not blossom, nor fruit be on the vines, the produce of the olive fail and the fields yield no food, the flock be cut off from the fold and there be no herd in the stalls, yet I will rejoice in the Lord; I will take joy in the God of my salvation. God, the Lord, is my strength; he makes my feet like a deer's; he makes me tread on my high places (Habakkuk 3:17-19 ESV).*

Habakkuk's prayer was on my heart moments before I was wheeled in for a mastectomy. I did not know how extensive the cancer was, nor if God was near to calling me home, but I resolved to praise

God no matter what the outcome. In that resolve, my soul was strengthened with peace and hope for a future regardless of what it held. By God's grace, Habakkuk's words strengthened my resolve to trust the Lover of My Soul—no matter what.

Further Investigation

Song: "Do I Trust You," by Twila Paris

Bible Passage: 1 Peter 1

Memory verse: *For all have sinned and fall short of the glory of God (Romans 3:23).*

Reflective activity: Take time to worship God in a garden or nature setting. Pen your own prayer to Him pouring out your soul like Habakkuk did.

Prayer:

Sovereign God,

With hope that will not disappoint, I look for the day when evil will be banished forever. Until that time, I will trust you to work all things for your glory and the good of my soul. I take joy in your salvation. You are my strength. Amen.

Living in the Now

This is what I have observed to be good: that it is appropriate for a person to eat, to drink and to find satisfaction in their toilsome labor under the sun during the few days of life God has given them—for this is their lot.

(Ecclesiastes 5:18 NIV)

With the past, I have nothing to do; nor with the future. I live now.

-Ralph Waldo Emerson

My germ radar was up. Most of the restaurant booths were filled. I heard several people coughing. In my world that translated into potential danger. The closer my contact with people, the more risk of infection I had due to my low white blood cell count. Chemotherapy destroys fast growing cells like cancer, but it also kills other fast growing cells like white blood cells. My white cell count was so low that simple infections could cause major issues. Gathering with several of my girlfriends for lunch was a special treat, but being in public was risky. I eyed the salt shaker and wondered how many people had touched it. Seasoned food was worth the risk; I picked it up.

"So how was your last chemo treatment?" Joan asked me as she poured Honey Mustard dressing on her salad.

"OK," I mumbled between bites full of chicken. I wasn't supposed to eat salad in restaurants like the other ladies were eating. My food needed to be well cooked.

"You look good," she continued.

"Thanks!"

"So do your treatments make you sick?"

"Yes, for the first week. I'm feeling better now; however, my white cell count is pretty low. That's the thing. Just when I feel better, I have to be careful in social settings because my white cell count is low. By the time my white cell count comes back up, it's time for another session of chemo."

"Wow! That sounds hard," she sympathized.

"Well, it could be much worse," I answered, remembering the cases of chemo reactions I had heard about.

"So what happens when you go in for your chemo sessions? Tell me about them," she continued.

I took a deep breath, and decided to be bluntly honest. "You know, I don't really want to talk about my chemotherapy sessions. They aren't fun. I try not to think about them in between sessions. I just want to live *now* by enjoying being here with you ladies. Tell me what is happening with you. How is God meeting you?"

"Good to know," she answered as her eyes filled with compassionate tears.

Conversation steered away from cancer and its treatments, and I relaxed and focused on something other than my current hardships. I was learning how to live in the moment. Remembering the past made me wish I were well again. Thinking about the future could be scary. But I have this day right now to live. This luncheon was an opportunity to be with friends who were dear to me. If I listened to them instead of thinking of my own problems, I could participate in their lives through encouragement and prayer. When our conversation focused on things of God, my soul was soothed in the midst of suffering. It reminded me of a song I had learned as a child.

> *We have this moment to hold in our hands*
>
> *And to touch as it slips through our fingers like sand*
>
> *Yesterday's gone and tomorrow may never come,*
>
> *but we have this moment today (Gaither).*

Learning to treasure each moment that God gives includes: paying attention to the details at hand; taking worry thoughts captive; counting blessings; making the most of the current opportunity; and fulfilling my God-given purpose each day. Chemotherapy and cancer would be conquered one day at a time. Sometimes I had to break time down into even smaller units—one hour at a time—or one injection at a time.

Stretches of every day have pockets of happiness; I was determined to bathe in those *joy puddles*. This would take self-disciplined thought and a focus on gratitude, but it could be done. Instead of simply enduring the difficult times, I searched for meaning and purpose both in my current moments and their potential eternal impact.

Live with Purpose

Living in the now means we are focused on the purpose of the present moment. It is not contrary to living with an eternal focus because when our focus is eternal, the present becomes priceless. When we realize that what happens in each moment on earth affects eternity, the value of the present tense becomes an everlasting treasure.

Each day's purpose has eternal impact. An encouraging word offered to an elderly nursing home patient may be written in an eternal book. A child in Sunday school who decides to follow Jesus today will spend eternity with Him in Heaven. We must never underestimate the eternal significance and power of walking moment by moment with the Holy Spirit.

When we face difficulties, it is easy to forget that each moment in time has purpose in God's plan. We can get so focused on our pain that we forget our purpose. Finding purpose in our pain, however, strengthens our faith.

If our health creates the need for physical rest, we can find purpose in abiding time with Jesus—drawing nearer to His heart through prayer and the study of His Word. When we need help from our brothers and sisters in Christ, we remember that God is teaching how to give and receive the gifts of service and love. In the grieving moments of death, we rest in the one who conquered death by giving us eternal life in Jesus Christ our Lord, and we glory in the hope of eternal reunion with those we love.

We are God's witnesses, and during times of crises we are being watched. People wonder if we will walk our talk. Even the simple act of clinging to Jesus during painful moments of our lives has eternal impact on those around us. When we see God's faithfulness to others, we trust that He will also be there in our times of sorrow and suffering.

Jesus offers the key to our life purpose in the two greatest commandments. *"You shall love the Lord your God with all your heart and with all your soul and with all your mind. This is the great and first commandment. And a second is like it: You shall love your neighbor as yourself (Matthew 22: 37-39).* Times of crises are intense times that often stop the flurry of life's activity and make us focus on what is really important—the eternal bond of love.

Each morning we ask God to lead our day in love, and each night we reflect: Did I bless someone else today despite my own pain? Was there purpose in this day other than survival? Did I walk closer with my God? Did I offer a cup of water to anyone in the name of Jesus? How might my current condition be of use to the kingdom? How can I best glorify God even in this difficult situation? God has a purpose for us in every hardship we face, and we want to fulfill that purpose. Instead of focusing on our pain, we should focus on God's purpose for our pain.

Take Every Thought Captive

Living in the now means we focus on the present as it relates to an eternal purpose. We don't dwell on the past or worry about a future that may never happen. We learn to enjoy the moments we are given. We focus on the giving of thanks and joy. This requires taking our thoughts captive through the Holy Spirit's power.

God grants us power to control our thoughts, channeling them down paths of righteousness. When worry for the future sets in, we change our thought patterns much like we would change the channel on the TV.

This doesn't mean that we just decide not to think about a destructive thought pattern. Trying to ignore something only makes us think about it more. We need to replace harmful thoughts with holy thoughts, so we change our thinking to dwell on things that are true, honorable, right, pure, lovely, of good reputation, excellent, and worthy of praise (Philippians 4:8).

For example, if our thought pattern has been focusing on fears about the future, we instead focus on our eternal purpose in the given moment. How can I impact eternity now? Eternal impact comes from being satisfied with God, regardless of our circumstance. Positive thoughts may include a meditation on God's character, reliance in His trust, or faith in His purposes.

In his book *Desiring God;* John Piper explains "God is most glorified in us when we are most satisfied in him." Finding satisfaction in God with our present circumstances brings Him glory. Satisfaction in God can be as simple as gratitude for the moment He gives. We live in the moment by noticing the details of His creation and giving thanks. Enjoy the company of those around you. Laugh freely, love with passion, and make the most of the moment's opportunity. These actions are products of our satisfaction in God and His plan.

Another possibility would be to replace our fears with the hope of eternal joy. Visualization is one way to meditate on eternity with God. Take time to imagine what Heaven is like. Find joy in the glory of life with no more sorrow, pain, suffering, sin, or death. Give thanks to the one who died for you so that you could spend eternity with Him. Instead of fearing the future on earth, glory in the future of Heaven.

God gives us His divine power to wage war against the strongholds of our mind. We can destroy arguments and lofty opinions that are raised against the knowledge of God (2 Corinthians 10:4-5). God also gives us weapons in this war for our mind: prayer, the Word of God, faith, and the power of the indwelling Holy Spirit. Through Christ, we have the power to control our thoughts, taking them captive through the weapons of our warfare. We learn to focus our thoughts on the present circumstance in the light of thanksgiving and with an eternal hope for the future.

Live Like We Are Dying

Grass that withers, flowers that fade, vapors of mist—these are all things that life on earth is compared to in Scripture. What should be most important to us today is what would be most important if this were our last day on earth. By living in the moment, we don't assume that we will have a tomorrow on earth. Life is short, sometimes much shorter than we realize. We must focus on living it fully: absorbing every moment of God-given pleasure, making the most of every opportunity, dwelling in peace, searching for joy, and remaining content in whatever circumstance we find ourselves. We trust our Sovereign God.

Life is uncertain, but on a daily basis, we seldom remember this truth. We live each day as if life on earth would never end. When in crisis, we realize that our life on earth truly is a vapor. This realization creates urgency for right relationship with God and people. We are more likely to love freely and fiercely.

The urgency of time wakes us from our complacency to a life of purpose. Reconciliation with a son would be critical to prevent him from storming off in a car that might never come home. Words of love would flow more freely to elderly parents if we realized that this encounter might be our last. Searching for opportunity, we would share the love of Christ with our neighbor because we might not have another chance. We would not withhold our affections, for tomorrow might not come. The only treasures of earth that we can take with us into eternity are people; therefore, loving others is essential to our purpose on earth. Times of crises can teach us how to love with purpose.

We need to ask ourselves: What words would I say if today were my last day on earth? Who would I hug? Who would I call? With whom would I share Christ? If we commune intimately with the Holy Spirit and live each day as if it were our last, our lives will fulfill their purpose and be fully satisfied in any circumstance.

Make the Most of Every Opportunity

While we are in difficult times, we often tend to focus on the future with the hope that things will be better. If that future hope is Heaven, then those thoughts are worthwhile, but if we are focusing on a time when life will be better on earth, we are in danger of exchanging today for a future we may never have. We lose the opportunities of love that present themselves this day.

When we live in the present with an eternal perspective, we learn to make the most of every opportunity. We watch for opportunities that develop from the most difficult times of our lives. Why did God give us this difficult road? We are God's witnesses. When we go through difficult times, we are being watched. People wonder: Will our faith remain solid? Will our God see us through? Do we have a faith that weathers the drought and storm, or is it a fair weather faith? Is our faith passionate, even in the midst of sorrow, because we have a hope for eternity?

My mother-in-law, Ardith, is purposeful about watching for opportunities to glorify God in all circumstances. One Sunday afternoon after eating fried chicken, Ardith was suddenly rushed to the emergency room with severe abdominal pain. Her gallbladder was immediately removed, and because of infection she had to stay in the hospital. She shared a room with Shaunta, an eighteen year old girl who had Sickle Cell Anemia.

Shaunta told Ardith all about her difficult life, and Ardith listened well. Before Ardith left the hospital, she and Shaunta were good friends, and Shaunta had decided to become a follower of Christ.

Shaunta did not have a nurturing mother, so Ardith began to fill this gap for her. Shaunta would spend several days at a time at Ardith's house. Ardith cooked for her, listened to her heartaches, and loved her with the love of Christ. Shaunta began to grow in her love and knowledge of Jesus. The prognosis for Shauta's disease was grim; salvation in Christ gave Shaunta hope for eternal life after death.

While Ardith's gallbladder surgery was a one-time procedure, Shaunta was in and out of the hospital numerous times with her disease. One day the telephone rang, and Ardith received the news that she had long suspected would come. Shaunta was home with Jesus. Shaunta's mother wept as she told Ardith how grateful she was that Ardith had cared for her daughter. Ardith again made the most of the opportunity, and shared the love of Jesus with Shaunta's mother.

Ardith didn't know why God would allow a sudden gallbladder attack, but she trusted that God had a purpose in her pain. She watched for opportunities to give God glory in her present situation. Through Ardith's watchful trust in God's plan, Shaunta's life on earth and eternal destination were changed. In the midst of her own hardship, Ardith was aware of the opportunities for the kingdom.

We, too, can impact eternity by watching for opportunities to share the love of Christ with others, even in our pain. The most difficult times of life are often platforms. People listen when we are in crisis because they want to find the source of the river of peace that flows through the soul of a follower of Christ during life's most difficult circumstances.

Be Content

My great-grandmother was one hundred four years old, and she was anticipating heaven with joy. Gangrene had set into her leg. Her last words to me were, "I am trying to be content." *Living in the now* means we are content in whatever circumstance we find ourselves. This doesn't mean that we have to be happy about our current condition, but rather that we trust God's greater purpose in allowing our struggle. We live in the now while searching for the opportunities that God presents for the good of His kingdom.

The Apostle Paul explained to the Philippians how he had learned to be content:

> *I have learned in whatever situation I am to be content. I know how to be brought low, and I know how to abound. In any and every circumstance, I have learned the secret of facing plenty and hunger, abundance and need. I can do all things through Christ who strengthens me (Philippians 4: 11-13 ESV).*

The power of contentment is driven by the strength that we find in Christ. Through Him, we can do anything He calls us to do including resting in godly contentment in any circumstance.

Paul further explained this idea to the Hebrews when He encouraged them to be content with what they had because God has said *I will never leave you nor forsake you (Hebrews 13:5 ESV)*. If all else is taken from us: our health, finances, home, or even those we love—we know that we still have God. He is with us always and will never leave us. He will give us the strength to endure the most difficult times of our lives.

With the Holy Spirit's presence comes His eternal promise of restoration. Life on earth is short; Heaven will be gloriously eternal. When we reach the shores of Heaven, there will be no more sorrow, pain, or death. In that promise we can rest contentedly. The present difficult circumstance will not last forever. God be praised!

Focus

Learning to *live in the now* takes focus. We pay attention to what is happening in the moment we are living; we notice the details. We watch for God working and for opportunities to give Him glory. We enjoy the immediate pleasures before us.

Part of focus is countering fears, worries, or negative thinking with truths from God's Word. We consciously turn our thoughts from negative patterns and mediate on the truth of God's Word that we have hidden in our hearts through memorization and meditation.

When fear of the future looms, we pray through our anxieties and focus on the task at hand, willing ourselves to live in the moment. We miss so much of life if we don't live in the present. If we are focused on our past or worried for our future, today's joys escape us. God's grace is sufficient for the day. He does not give us His grace to worry about what may come. And whatever comes—He is already there preparing the way for us.

Cancer and its treatment taught me the importance of living in the now. I realized for the first time that my life on earth could be near the end. I didn't know how much time I had left with those that I loved. An even stranger realization was that this is true for all of us. None of us knows how long we will live on earth. Several people who were apparently healthy while I was going through chemo treatments are no longer with us. They had no idea that their life would soon end.

Life is a vapor. We must live each moment with purpose—making the most of every opportunity at hand. Regardless of what we are going through, we must take the time each day to offer thanks, breathe deeply of the fragrances of life, love those with whom we share life, and walk intimately with our God.

Further Investigation

Song: "We Have This Moment Today," Gaither Vocal Band

Bible Passage: Ephesians 5:15-20

Memory Verse: *Behold, what I have seen to be good and fitting is to eat and drink and find enjoyment in all the toil with which one toils under the sun the few days of his life that God has given him, for this is his lot (Ecclesiastes 5:18 ESV).*

Reflective question: How might *living in the now* help me to endure a difficult time?

Prayer:

Lord God,

Help me to focus on the pleasures at hand. Help me to focus on the small gifts and joys of life. Tune my heart to listen well, to love much, and to search for doors of opportunity to love you and those around me in every circumstance of life. Help my heart to be content right where I am—here *in the now.* Amen.

Grace upon Grace

And from his fullness we have all received, grace upon grace.

(John 1:16 ESV)

Amazing grace, how sweet the sound that saved a wretch like me,
I once was lost, but now am found, was blind, but now I see.

"Amazing Grace," by John Newton

    The blood of slaves and cries for justice haunted the memories of John Newton. Did the suffering groans of those chained in ships waken him from his sleep? As Newton threw those infected with smallpox and dysentery into the sea, did the ocean depths that engulfed their diseased bodies also threaten to drown Newton's diseased soul? Newton never forgot the atrocities of slave trade: the buying, selling, and bartering of human beings; he had been the commander of an English slave ship.

    Newton's vessel would anchor off the African coast waiting for the delivery of slaves captured in raids and wars. Chained human cargo on slave ships had a mortality rate of twenty percent or higher. Newton was the cause of inhumane suffering and torturous death for generations of people.

During a powerful storm at sea, Newton's ship was nearly lost. Desperately, he cried out to Jesus for the rescue not only of his flailing ship, but of his heart flailing in its own gale of guilt.

Although forgiven by the Savior, Newton never forgot the depth of his sins or the consequences of suffering that he had caused. He preached the gospel for forty-three years after he forsook the slave trade, yet his tombstone's confession and saving proclamation reads: *Once an infidel and libertine, a servant of slaves in Africa, was, by the rich mercy of our Lord and Savior Jesus Christ, preserved, restored, pardoned, and appointed to preach the faith he had long labored to destroy.*

John Newton understood the deep truths of God's grace and forgiveness. He knew the wretchedness of his sins—torturous treachery against humans and God. He called himself a wretch saved by grace. The melodies of his forgiven and grateful heart continue to sing out through the generations in the beloved hymn that he penned, *Amazing Grace*. What exactly is this grace of which Newton sang?

Long before Newton, there was a woman who also realized the depth of the depravity of her soul and the saving power of God's grace. God did not see fit to reveal her specific sins in Scripture, only that she was known to be a sinner. Perhaps the vagueness of her guilt encourages each of us to ponder our own acts of iniquity against God's laws of love. Certainly, instead of condemning her, we should examine our own heart.

Imagine this woman, scorned by society, entering the fellowship of the proud and elite Pharisees. In complete humility, she drops to her knees before Jesus pouring out her heart of repentance to the one who loves her unconditionally. The Pharisees' self-righteousness contrasts sharply with the woman's wholehearted and genuine repentance and overflowing heart of gratitude. *...and standing behind him at his feet, weeping, she began to wet his feet with her tears and wiped them with the hair of her head and kissed his feet and anointed them with the ointment (Luke 7:38 ESV).*

The Pharisees were astounded that Jesus allowed this woman to even touch Him. Her sins were well known. Yet her actions demonstrated her faith, repentance, and love for her Savior. Contrary to the Pharisees, she understood that Jesus was full of grace and that out of His fullness she could also receive grace upon grace (John 1:14 & 16).

Jesus responded to the Pharisees. *Therefore I tell you, her sins, which are many, are forgiven (Luke 7:47a ESV).* Then full of grace and compassion, Jesus told the woman: *"Your sins are forgiven." "Your faith has saved you; go in peace." (Luke 7:48 & 7:50 ESV).* This story portrays the truth of Ephesians 2:8-9: *For by grace you have been saved through faith. And this is not your own doing; it is the gift of God, not a result of works, so that no one may boast (ESV).*

Lest we be like the Pharisees, we must examine our own souls to find the wretchedness within. Do we think John Newton's sins were worse than the depravity of our own heart? One sin alone would be enough to keep us from the presence of God and our eternal home if it were not for God's grace. The Book of James tells us: *For whoever keeps the whole law and yet stumbles in one point, he has become guilty of all (James 2:10 NASB).* Let us fall before Jesus broken by the wretchedness of our own degeneracy like the woman who fell before Jesus. Each of us needs to be rescued by the amazing grace that is a free gift of undeserved mercy and love.

The undeserved mercy and love of God is what sent Jesus to the cross in our place to take the penalty for our sins, but grace doesn't end at salvation. The undeserved mercy of God meets us moment by moment. While grace allowed a slave trader eternal redemption, it also gave him the power to change his life.

Newton was not the only recipient of grace on his slave ship. Grace abounds for all who call on Christ. Those held captive on John Newton's ship, those who suffered at Newton's hands, had the same offer of grace and love. We can trust that the God who strengthens and sustains whispered messages of eternal hope to His beloved, those enslaved believers who endured torturous suffering at the hands of Newton.

Through grace, God meets us in our sorrows. Grace is the reason God walks with us day to day, strengthening and encouraging our souls. Grace sustains us no matter what comes. God proclaims that His grace is sufficient for our every need. While grace does not always take away our pain, it provides a way for God to walk with us in our pain. Grace sustains us in a world gone awry and leads us to our eternal home.

Grace, the undeserved love and mercy of God, is the root of everything good in our lives.

A Life of Grace

Stephen was a man full of grace according to the Book of Acts. As a martyr, Stephen portrayed grace in the face of persecution and death. He was known for his demonstrations of great wonders and signs; consequently, enemies of Christ became enemies of Stephen. These enemies instigated lies about Stephen; eventually, he was dragged before the high council.

As the council interrogated Stephen, they could not help but notice a manifestation of God's grace. Stephen's countenance looked like the face of an angel. This same grace allowed Stephen to speak boldly to the council. Filled with the Holy Spirit, Stephen recounted the historical working of God among the Israelite people and held them accountable for their unbelief. *"You stiff-necked people, uncircumcised in heart and ears, you always resist the Holy Spirit,"* Stephen declared (Acts 7:51 ESV). Furious, the crowd gnashed their teeth, but God's grace did abound. Stephen, *full of the Holy Spirit, gazed into heaven and saw the glory of God, and Jesus standing at the right hand of God. And he said, "Behold, I see the Heavens opened, and the Son of Man standing at the right hand of God" (Acts 7:55-56 ESV).*

Further enraged, Stephen's persecutors covered their ears, cried out with loud voices, and rushed upon Stephen. They cast him out of the city and stoned him to death. God's grace still did not fall short. As Stephen was dying, grace allowed forgiveness to reign. Stephen asked God to forgive the people for their sin. In Stephen's darkest hour, grace triumphed to the very threshold of eternity.

The Apostle Paul also endured much suffering for the sake of Christ. Paul marveled at the strange dichotomy of grace that abounds in suffering when he declared *when I am weak, then I am strong (2 Corinthians 12:10b ESV).*

Chosen by God, the Apostle Paul's conversion was dramatic. It included brilliant light, a voice from Heaven, and temporary blindness. Though Paul was called by God in a spectacular conversion, he knew the temptations of his own heart. One of those temptations was conceit.

Paul said that to keep him from being conceited, God allowed a thorn in the flesh to harass him. This thorn was delivered by the messenger Satan, but was allowed by God. Three times Paul asked God to take away his suffering, but God's response was, "*My grace is sufficient for you, for my power is made perfect in weakness*" *(2 Corinthians 12:9 ESV).*

Paul learned that in weakness and humility, grace abounds. When we know we are weak, we lean on the strength of God's grace. If we abound in our own strength, failure is certain. Paul was content with insults, hardships, persecutions, and even calamities because he knew that when he was weak, he could lean on the grace of God to provide true strength. How might we, like Stephen or the Apostle Paul, learn to lean on the all-sufficient grace of God in every hardship? What exactly, does grace help us to do?

Grace Allows Us to Believe

For the grace of God has appeared that offers salvation to all people (Titus 2:11 NIV). Grace—the unmerited mercy, favor, and love of God—is what allows us to be drawn to Him. In love, and despite our betrayals and deceit, God draws us to himself (John 6:44). We do not become children of God by the good that we do, but by accepting God's mercy (Titus 3:5). This is a mercy that causes God to hold out His hands all day long to obstinate people (Romans 10:21). The heart of God says, "Come home, child. You are precious in my sight. I love you" (Isaiah 43:4). He offers the free gift of salvation to all who will receive it (Romans 6:23). A gift given in grace.

Grace Fills Us with the Holy Spirit's Power

Stephen relied completely on God's strength to speak boldly for Christ in the face of imminent persecution and death. Having been filled with the Holy Spirit's power, Stephen was enabled to fulfill God's purpose even in the face of persecution; he was a powerhouse for God.

God's grace empowers us to do anything God calls us to do. This includes glorifying God during difficult times of our lives. The Apostle Paul explained it like this: *I can do all things through Christ who strengthens me (Philippians 4:13 NKJV).*

The Holy Spirit's power is often thought about in terms of miracles, but the Apostle Paul said that the Holy Spirit had empowered him to be content. What if we don't receive a miracle? Does that mean God's grace and the Holy Spirit's power are not present? Contentment is a moment-to-moment reliance on God. The Holy Spirit's power and grace are demonstrated in the quiet strength of the ones who are suffering.

Anything that happens to us passes through the hands of God, and the Holy Spirit walks with us through every trial. Moment by moment, the Spirit strengthens, encourages, and comforts us. Paul explained that even in the miseries of life, God's grace and the Holy Spirit's power enable us to be content in any situation. Contentment doesn't mean we have to like our circumstances, but rather that we trust God in them. Grace allows us to trust despite the pain.

Grace Provides Wisdom through the Holy Spirit's Guidance

As Stephen was dragged before the council, God's favor guided him in wisdom. Stephen spoke boldly for the sake of the Gospel, unafraid to speak the truth even though he knew it would likely mean his death. He was filled with the Holy Spirit as he eloquently presented his case to the council, and he didn't recant the truth which was the only hope for their souls.

Like Stephen, when we humbly ask God for wisdom, He bestows it generously through the leading of the Holy Spirit. Wisdom allows clear decisions that glorify God and are for the good of His children. Wisdom even guides the details of life such as when to be silent or knowing which words would be most comforting or edifying. Wisdom reflects on a situation and plans the best course. It offers kindness and self-control when the world around us stampedes along a different path.

There is a difference between earthly wisdom and wisdom endowed by the grace of God. The grace of God allows us to have the wisdom to live life with simplicity and godly sincerity (2 Corinthians 1:12). When through grace the Spirit of God endows wisdom, it includes understanding, knowledge, and even craftsmanship (Exodus 31:3).

God's laws are wisdom for living. We can only follow them through the empowerment of the Holy Spirit. God's principles make us wise and compassionate people (Deuteronomy 4:6).

If we ask for wisdom, God promises to give it liberally (James 1:5). Wisdom reveals Jesus to us and gives us knowledge of Him (Ephesians 1:17). True wisdom is manifested in our behavior which will be pure, peaceable, gentle, reasonable, merciful, unwavering, and sincere (James 3:17). Because of God's grace, we can walk moment by moment in the wisdom of the Spirit.

Grace Offers Peace that Passes Understanding

Everyone who sat on the council, to which Stephen was dragged, gazed at him in amazement. Though he faced a crowd of tormentors, Stephen's countenance was like the face of an angel radiating peace and light. Filled with grace and power, Stephen was flooded with the peace that passes understanding, and that peace was physically visible.

When through God's grace we abide in His presence, we, too, can be flooded with peace that defies circumstance. This allows us to rejoice in the presence of God for He is ever near. In a spirit of prayer, and with a heart of thanksgiving, we continue to commune with God in the midst of chaos. With this rejoicing spirit, anxiety wanes, and our soul floods with a peace that even we cannot understand. It is a peace born of God's favor that guards our hearts and minds in Christ Jesus.

Grace Lets Us See God

As stones were hurled at Stephen, he saw God. *But he, full of the Holy Spirit, gazed into Heaven and saw the glory of God, and Jesus standing at the right hand of God. And he said, "Behold, I see the Heavens opened, and the Son of Man standing at the right hand of God."(Acts 7:55-56 ESV)*. As Stephen was being martyred for his faith in Christ, Jesus stood to welcome him home. In Stephen's last moments on earth, grace allowed Stephen to focus on Jesus and His everlasting kingdom.

Grace allows us to see God in the midst of our hardship, too. Just as Christ was aware of Stephen's pain, He is aware of ours. He stands ready and attentive to our call. He speaks to us in His Word, and He surrounds us with the comfort of the Holy Spirit. And one day He will welcome us home to His everlasting kingdom where there is no more sorrow, no more pain, no more tears, and no more death.

Grace Allows Us to Forgive

Stephen's last words were words of forgiveness. Just as Jesus offered undeserved mercy to Stephen, Stephen offered it to those who persecuted him.

In our pain, God's grace gives us the ability to forgive even in the most difficult situations. In forgiveness, we are freed from the chains of bitterness and rage that enslave us. Grace allows us to be renewed in the spirit of our minds. We focus our thoughts on all that is good, commendable, excellent, or worthy of praise. We put off our old self and put on a new self created in the likeness of God who is true, righteous and holy (Ephesians 4: 22-24).

Forgiveness does not mean we do not address the truth. Stephen certainly addressed truth as he called his persecutors stiff-necked people, uncircumcised in heart and ears, people who always resist the Holy Spirit (Acts 7:51). Yet, forgiveness lets go of bitterness, wrath, and malice. It offers kindness and tenderhearted care despite the wrong. Grace allows us to offer to others what Jesus offers to us—undeserved mercy.

Moment by Moment Grace

God crowns our life with goodness and kindness. His mercy follows us. Every perfect gift comes down from above. Because of His grace, we are not consumed. We have an anchor for our soul in the Rock that is Jesus—steady, sure, unfaltering. Grace gets us through each day, grace sees us through each storm, and grace will bring us safely home to the arms of Jesus.

Grace, the undeserved favor of God, leads us to repentance and belief in Jesus as our Savior. It gives us a boldness to do God's will. Signs and wonders are a result of God's grace, as is the wisdom to speak in the Spirit. Grace transforms us into people who radiate peace even in the midst of persecution because grace fills us with the Holy Spirit. Grace allows us to see God, and because we know we are forgiven, it allows us to forgive others. Because of grace, we have an inheritance that will never perish or fade—a place reserved in Heaven with our Savior, Jesus.

One day all of life's hardships will be over, and like Stephen, we will see the face of God. As we contemplate our lives, we will see God's hand of grace every step of the way—leading, guiding, consoling, and encouraging. Perhaps we will then sing:

> *Wonderful the matchless grace of Jesus,*
>
> *Deeper than the mighty rolling sea;*
>
> *Wonderful grace, all sufficient for me, for even me.*
>
> *Broader than the scope of my transgressions,*
>
> *Greater far than all my sin and shame,*
>
> *O magnify the precious Name of Jesus.*
>
> *Praise His Name!*
>
> *("Wonderful Grace of Jesus" by Haldor Lilenas 1885-1959)*

Further Investigation

Songs: "Amazing Grace," by John Newton and "Wonderful Grace of Jesus," by Haldor Lilenas

Bible Passage: Acts 6 & 7 (Stephen)

Memory Verse: For by grace you have been saved through faith. And this is not your own doing; it is the gift of God, not a result of works, so that no one may boast (Ephesians 2:8-9 ESV).

Reflective question: How does grace manifest itself in your life?

Prayer:

God of Grace,

Thank you for your unmerited mercy that sent Jesus to the cross to die in my place. I know I do not deserve your favor, yet you look on me with love and kindness every moment of every day. You fill my life with all that is good. I have so much for which to be thankful. Yes, even in my darkest night, your grace is sufficient for me. Please fill me with your Holy Spirit so that I may reflect grace to others even as you offer grace to me. Amen.

Peace That Passes Understanding

And the peace of God, which surpasses all understanding, will guard your hearts and your minds in Christ Jesus.
(Philippians 4:7 ESV)

God cannot give us a happiness and peace apart from Himself, because it is not there. There is no such thing. –C. S. Lewis

To will what God wills brings peace. –Amy Carmichael

Every part of me was pulled in tight. My knees and blanket were tucked under my chin. I pulled my pillow over my head to block out the audible reminders of pain. I did not want to hear the angry voices that were destroying the peace of our home and causing anxiety in my soul. Every muscle in my body felt achy with tension, and my head was throbbing as I wept into my pillow. Anxiety was gnawing at my stomach and coursing through my veins with each rapid heartbeat.

Surrounding my parents' divorce, custody battles were raging. Their tensions could be heard throughout the house in angry voices and slamming doors. The future loomed uncertain. Families weren't supposed to be torn apart like this leaving hearts broken into pieces seemingly beyond repair.

As a new believer, my heart cried out to Jesus. I poured out my fear and hurt to the lover of my soul and my only perfect parent. Like a tranquil pool settles a raft after a series of rapids, an unexplainable calm began to settle my thoughts and soothe my emotions. My muscles relaxed; my crying ceased. Tension subsided into background noise as I focused on Jesus. I remember thinking, "This is *the peace that passes understanding*. I have heard about this." I was experiencing the fulfillment of a promise of God. *The Lord is at hand; do not be anxious about anything, but in everything by prayer and supplication with thanksgiving let your requests be made known to God. And the peace of God, which surpasses all understanding, will guard your hearts and minds in Christ Jesus (Philippians 4:5-6 ESV).* Within moments I was asleep fulfilling yet another of God's precious truths. *In peace I will both lie down and sleep; for you alone, O Lord, make me dwell in safety (Psalm 4:8 ESV).*

What had happened? As a new believer and young teen-ager, I didn't know much theology. My prayer was a desperate cry heard by a loving Father. In love and compassion, my Abba Father, Daddy God, guarded my heart and mind just as He had promised He would do. That heartfelt cry to God was the beginning of an intimate relationship with my Jesus. I never forgot that night—a miracle in my soul that could not be explained.

Decades later, I seek God's peace intentionally. Experiencing peace in chaos is a process of taking fearful and worried thoughts captive and replacing them with the truths of God. It is a process of recognizing that worry changes nothing, but prayer taps into power that can change everything.

This power enables us to overcome negative emotions through the Holy Spirit of God. Is this an easy process? No, it is a battlefield of the mind. We fight in the power of the Holy Spirit using the weapons of God. *In all circumstances take up the shield of faith, with which you can extinguish all the flaming darts of the evil one; and take the helmet of salvation, and the sword of the Spirit, which is the word of God, praying at all times in the Spirit, with all prayer and supplication (Ephesians 6:16-18a ESV).* When we let our minds dwell on God's truth and promises, focusing on His character and sovereignty instead of our troubles, peace prevails.

One way to focus on God is to spend time with Him in nature. Jesus modeled this by going to the Garden of Gethsemane, the wilderness, and desolate places to pray. Absorbing God's beauty all around us focuses our thoughts on the Creator. While spending time in nature, we can intentionally quiet our body and mind as a prerequisite to quieting our soul. In a spirit of thanks, we meditate on the grandeur of creation which displays God's power, might, and His awesome works. In this quiet, our soul can begin to rest so we can listen to the Holy Spirit.

As we listen, God often speaks to us by bringing to mind Scripture passages, hymns, and eternal truths. Praying over the Word in a nature retreat is a powerful means of soaking in truth that promotes peace.

When our soul rests in trust, God's peace prevails. Peace is the result of trusting God, regardless of the circumstance or emotions. Getting to this point of trust requires intentional time to abide with God.

Recently, *the peace that passes understanding* was evident in my friend, Katie. Twenty-six weeks into her pregnancy, Katie was in a motorcycle accident. Her foot and ankle were mangled, and the trauma of the accident started contractions which were threatening her baby. As Katie rode in the ambulance after the accident, she remembered that my youngest daughter, Taylor, was born at twenty-five weeks gestation. Remembering the miracle of Taylor gave Katie hope in a God of miracles.

When I visited Katie in the hospital, doctors were focusing on limb salvage while preventing her baby's premature birth. Katie, an active athlete, ran four miles a day even while pregnant; now she was in danger of losing her foot. She faced delicate surgery that would require hours of anesthesia. It would be a difficult balance between saving Katie's foot and protecting the baby from the anesthesia and necessary pain medications.

Despite all this, Katie radiated peace. When I first entered her hospital room, she smiled and took my hand. Her countenance was relaxed—even joyful! God's peace pervaded. "I am glad to have the chance to glorify God in difficult circumstances," Katie gently explained to me. Her sweet spirit of trust and peace in God bolstered my own faith.

After several weeks in the hospital undergoing hours of delicate reconstruction surgeries and skin grafts, Katie went home. Her baby is doing well, and her foot is healing. Still, she has a long road ahead of her. Katie knows that Jesus will be with her on that road, and that knowledge brings her peace.

It truly is possible to have peace in the midst of chaos, but it isn't always instantaneous. It is a process of abiding through prayer and Scripture meditation as we turn our anxieties over to God.

Inner Peace is a Byproduct of Peace with God

Inner peace is a byproduct of intimate fellowship with God through Jesus Christ. Jesus is the Prince of Peace predicted by the prophet Isaiah (Isaiah 9:6). In fact, Jesus himself *is* our peace for He has reconciled us to God through the cross (Ephesians 2:14-16). Christ's righteousness is imputed to those who repent and believe in His name; therefore, in God's eyes we have the righteousness of Christ which allows close fellowship with the Father. Jesus broke down the barriers created by our sin, and He became our peace offering with God. The peace that Jesus offers is not like the world's peace which is conditional; God's peace transcends circumstance. Jesus said, "*. . . in me you may have peace. In the world you will have tribulation. But take heart; I have overcome the world*" (John 16:33 ESV).

Peace through Prayer and Thanksgiving

We allow God's peace to reign in our soul when we take our requests to Him in a spirit of thanksgiving. We change our thinking by taking our thoughts captive through prayer and gratitude. When we begin to worry, we tell Jesus our concerns and relinquish them to His control and purposes. Instead of mentally rehearsing our fears, we dwell in thanks and cast our troubles on the Burden Bearer because He cares for us. This process helps us to replace our anxious thoughts with gratitude. For what are we grateful? What do we know to be true, honorable, lovely, and excellent (Philippians 4:8)? In a spirit of prayer, we thank God for the details of blessing.

When I was going through chemotherapy, I tried to remember to thank God for all of His blessings in the midst of pain. Focusing on gratitude channeled my thoughts away from my miseries. When I dealt with the chemotherapy side effects of nausea, exhaustion, and hair loss, I thanked God for medications that killed fast-growing cancer cells. Though difficult to tolerate, these medicines would allow me more time on earth to raise my daughters. Nurses who were able to insert a needle intravenously on the first attempt were a special blessing because my veins were small and difficult to find. Though fatigued, my aching body and pounding head had a soft bed and pillow with plenty of blankets to cover me when I was chilled. My heart was overwhelmed with gratitude for the people who cared for me. Cards, phone calls, visits, meals—my life would abound with the blessings of Jesus through the hands and feet of His people.

One of my greatest joys was writing thank you cards. People would often tell me not to expend energy writing thank you notes, but they didn't realize that writing thank you notes was healing to my soul. Many times I wept as I wrote notes of gratitude to those who poured out their love to me in the name of Jesus. Gratitude settled my soul in peace and contentment instead of striving against the conditions that could not be changed.

Peace attained by abiding with God in prayer is an ancient truth. Thousands of years ago, King Jehoshaphat fought his fears with prayer and thanksgiving. The Moabites, Ammonites, and the people of Mount Seir were coming against him in battle. *Then Jehoshaphat was afraid and set his face to seek the Lord, and proclaimed a fast throughout all Judah. And Judah assembled to seek help from the Lord; from all the cities of Judah they came to seek the Lord (2 Chronicles 20:3-4 ESV).* Jehoshaphat's prayer began by praising God's sovereignty and power. *"O Lord, God of our fathers, are you not God in Heaven? You rule over all the kingdoms of the nations. In your hand are power and might, so that none is able to withstand you (2 Chronicles 20: 6 ESV).* Jehoshaphat then spent time remembering all that God had done for him in the past. He proclaimed his faith in God regardless of the circumstances they faced. *"If disaster comes upon us, the sword, judgment, or pestilence, or famine, we will stand before this house and before you—for your name is in this house—and cry out to you in our affliction, and you will hear and save." (2 Chronicles 20: 9 ESV).* Finally, Jehoshaphat detailed their troubles and asked God for help. In humility, Jehoshaphat acknowledged the Israelite's powerlessness and reiterated his faith in God. *"For we are powerless against this great horde that is coming against us. We do not know what to do, but our eyes are on you." (2 Chronicles 20:12 ESV).*

God heard and answered Jehoshaphat's prayer. The first thing our loving God addressed was Jehoshaphat's emotions. *"Do not be afraid and do not be dismayed at this great horde, for the battle is not yours but God's." (2 Chronicles 20: 15b ESV).* King Jehoshaphat's faith was strengthened when he was reminded that God was ultimately in control of all circumstances. Jehoshaphat fought his emotional and physical battles in the strength of prayer, and the result was peace.

Peace Through the Word

Peace comes when we pray through the truth and promises of Scripture and claim them as our own. We find Scriptures that are especially meaningful and memorize them so that we can meditate on them throughout the day. As followers of Christ, we have the Holy Spirit who comforts our souls with God's peace by breathing life into the Word so that it becomes a personal letter from God to us.

The Book of Psalms explains the peace that comes through meditation on the Word. *Great peace have those who love your law; nothing can make them stumble (Psalm 119: 165 ESV).* When we focus on God through the Word, He keeps us in perfect peace because meditation on God increases our faith and trust in the everlasting Rock (Isaiah 26:3-4). Peace is a product of the truth of Scripture embedded in our soul which allows us to abound in hope through the power of the Holy Spirit.

God's Peace Guards Our Hearts and Minds

The Apostle Paul told the Philippians that God's peace guards our hearts and minds in Christ Jesus (Philippians 4:7). When we trust the ways of God, even when we do not understand them, peace abides. Peace guards our minds from negative and harmful thoughts seeded by doubt or fear. When our mind is stayed on God, we ward off the thoughts that war with God's truth.

Faith and fear are opposite poles. When we abide with Jesus through prayer and study of the Word, faith is bolstered and fear diminishes allowing peace to reign.

Anger is another strong emotion that wars with peace. Though righteous anger gives us the strength to right a wrong, much anger is self-focused and is a result of emotional turmoil that does not get its own way. Focusing on God's principles convicts us of inappropriate anger and displaces it with peace. Peace does not co-exist with fear, anxiety, or unrighteous anger, so they vanish when peace prevails.

Thoughts and emotions are guarded by Jesus through his perfect peace.

The Apostle Paul told the Colossians to *Let the peace of Christ rule in your hearts. . . (Colossians 3:15 ESV)*. We must *let* peace reign. We prevent the peace of God from ruling when we focus on our worries, anxieties, and fears. When we let our minds dwell on our circumstance instead of God's truth, we allow chaos to enter our soul. We must open the gate to our heart and soul to Christ through prayer, meditation on the Word, and thanksgiving. Once the gate is open, God's peace is allowed to rush in much like water bursting forth from a dam release. Peace sooths, refreshes, and washes away worry, doubt, and fear.

Obedience Brings Peace

When we are obedient to the Holy Spirit, the God of Peace walks with us. *What you have learned and received and heard and seen in me—practice these things, and the God of peace will be with you (Philippians 4:9 ESV)*. Sometimes a lack of peace demonstrates that we are not listening to the guidance of the Holy Spirit. If we are disobedient, peace will elude us. Other times we do not have peace because we are wrestling with strong emotions like doubt, fear, or anger. When this happens, our act of obedience is prayer and meditation on God and his Word. In obedience, we take our emotions to God in ardent prayer.

Many times believers beat themselves up over their emotions adding guilt to an already emotion-laden situation. In life's trials, we will struggle with doubt, fear, or anger. Scriptures record times of fear and doubt in many of the patriarchs. Certainly, Jesus himself fought strong negative emotions by praying in the Garden of Gethsemane.

Emotion is not a sin—what we do with that emotion is critical. If fear gives way to worry, we are inappropriately handling it. If fear leads to prayer or meditation on God and His Word, then we are being obedient to God. Battling negative emotion with prayer is exactly what God tells us to do, and eventually peace will prevail. Often it is like fighting many battles in a war, however. Peace may prevail, and then another situation arises that rocks our faith, and fear returns. Each time we face negative thoughts and emotions, we battle them with prayer and the truths of God. When fear hits or doubts assail, we pray immediately. As long as we are praying through the negative emotions, we are doing exactly what God tells us to do.

Jacob wrestled with God in prayer when Jacob was afraid of his encounter with his brother, Esau (Genesis 32). After spending twenty years with Laban, Jacob's father-in-law, God told Jacob to return to the land of his father, Isaac. God promised to be with Jacob on the journey, but Jacob was afraid of Esau who had threatened to kill him years earlier. Jacob walked intimately with God, and God had faithfully protected and led Jacob through many disagreements and troubles with his father-in-law, Laban. Still, Jacob was afraid and distressed.

Jacob took his fears to God and asked for God's favor and protection for his family. *Save me, I pray, from the hand of my brother Esau, for I am afraid he will come and attack me, and also the mothers with their children (Genesis 32:11 NIV).* The prophet Hosea says Jacob wrestled God with tears and supplications (Hosea 12:4). Jacob fought his emotional battle by prayer.

In many ways, that is exactly what we do in prayer. We wrestle with God until we are in complete submission to His will and His ways. We wrestle until our souls rest in trust in God's ways—trusting that He knows what is best.

The Myth of Control

Sometimes the battle we are waging in prayer is a battle for control. We want our life to go a certain way, and God has other plans. God's ways do not always seem pleasant, and often we do not understand them. Like Jesus who was full of sorrow in the Garden of Gethsemane, we must get to a point where our soul response is, *"My Father, if it be possible, let this cup pass from me; nevertheless, not as I will, but as you will." (Matthew 26:39 ESV).*

Sometimes life has to be completely off-kilter before we recognize that we have believed the myth that *we* have control of our lives. Although we are dwarfed by the universe, we tell ourselves that we can control our world, but in reality chaos is all around us and threatens to consume us. We are not the ones in control of our world; God is. And for that we should be very grateful. When life is chaotic and we have no control, God still reigns. Peace often comes when we relinquish control to the one who knows better than we do what is best for the good of our soul.

When we relinquish control to God, we are demonstrating that in obedience we will follow God's guidance and trust Him with the results because He is worthy of our trust. God's compassion and love for us are greater than any other love we will experience. *If God is for us, who can be against us (Romans 8:31 ESV)?* When we trust the one who reigns over all, we will abide in peace. Even when life seems out of control, peace can reign when we rest in the truth of His sovereignty, trusting that everything He allows has a purpose for His glory and our good.

Peace in Times of Suffering

Experiencing peace doesn't mean that we won't have pain or sorrow. In our heartaches and heart breaks, we don't ignore our emotional upheaval, but rather talk to God about the grief and burdens we suffer.

The Apostle Paul encourages us to not lose heart in our suffering. *We are afflicted in every way, but not crushed; perplexed, but not driven to despair; persecuted, but not forsaken; struck down, but not destroyed;. . .(2 Corinthians 4:8-9 ESV).* Paul explains that even in the midst of life's most difficult circumstances, we do not despair because we have the peace of God in our soul. Even when we are perplexed and do not understand God's ways, we do not despair because we trust in God's sovereign plan. In persecution, we remember that we are never forsaken by God. The Apostle Paul further explained: *So we do not lose heart. Though our outer self is wasting away, our inner self is being renewed day by day (2 Corinthians 4:16 ESV).*

Peace; Be Still

Jesus demonstrated peace in the midst of chaos. Jesus' disciples were with Him on a boat when a great storm arose on the sea. The waves were breaking over the boat and it was filling with water. The disciples were amazed that in the midst of the chaos, Jesus was still asleep on a cushion in the stern. With the storm breaking around them, the disciples' fear of drowning was their overpowering thought. Overwhelmed, the disciples concluded that Jesus didn't care about them or their circumstance. They asked Him, *"Teacher, do you not care that we are perishing?" (Mark 4:38b ESV).*

Jesus woke and rebuked the wind and sea, *"Peace! Be Still!" (Mark 4:39 NKJV).* The winds ceased and there was great calm. Jesus then turned to His disciples and questioned their faith. *"Why are you so afraid? Have you still no faith?"(Mark 4:40 ESV).*

When the storms of life rock our boat and threaten to drown us, perhaps we feel like Jesus is asleep. Like the disciples, we may conclude that Jesus does not care about us. Yet Jesus made it clear to the disciples that strong faith trusts in God's love amidst any storm. Jesus wants to speak peace into our storms, but the peace He most desires is the peace of our soul. The circumstances of our lives do not change the fact that God loves us and that He is in control even if our storms rage to the very brink of death. Even in the valley of the shadow of death, our soul can find peace in the hope that we will dwell in the house of the Lord forever (Psalm 23).

Horatio Spafford understood storms at sea and God's peace. Spafford was a wealthy lawyer and business person in Chicago in the 1860s. He was a friend of D. L. Moody and one of Moody's best known supporters. Life for Horatio Spafford; however, soon turned into a series of tragedies. His only son died of scarlet fever when the boy was only four years old. A year later, the Great Chicago Fire destroyed much of the city. Spafford owned much real estate on the shores of Lake Michigan. Every property that Spafford owned was destroyed by the fire.

These disasters were very difficult for Spafford and his family, so they decided to get away from Chicago for a holiday to assist Moody while he toured in Europe. Just before their departure to England, Spafford was suddenly delayed by business. Spafford's wife and four daughters continued on the sea voyage without Spafford, expecting him to join them later in England.

Nine days later, Spafford received a telegram from his wife who had arrived in Wales. "Saved alone. What shall I do..." the Ville de Havre, the ship the Spaffords had been on, had collided with an English vessel, Lochearn. Within twelve minutes of impact, the Ville de Havre sank. Two hundred twenty-six people drowned. Among those drowned were all of Spafford's children.

Spafford's wife, Anna, survived because a plank drifted beneath her unconscious body and kept her afloat. Still unconscious, Anna was picked up by the crew of Lochearn. Anna's last memory was of her children clinging to her on the ship and the waters tearing her infant from her arms.

In Anna's despair following the drowning of her children, she heard a voice from God, "You were spared for a purpose." She immediately remembered the words of a friend who had said to her, "It's easy to be grateful and good when you have so much, but take care that you are not a fair-weather friend to God." A fellow survivor of the collision, Pastor Weiss, quoted Anna as saying, "God gave me four daughters. Now they have been taken from me. Someday I will understand why."

Upon receiving the telegram from Anna, Horatio immediately set sail to be with her. At one point on the journey the captain called Horatio to the bridge. "A careful reckoning has been made," he said, "and I believe we are now passing the place where the de Havre was wrecked. The water is three miles deep." Horatio returned to his cabin and wrote the words to a hymn that has been the heart's cry of hurting saints for hundreds of years:

> *It Is Well With My Soul*
>
> *When peace like a river, attendeth my way,*
>
> *When sorrows like sea billows roll;*
>
> *Whatever my lot, Thou has taught me to say,*
>
> *It is well, it is well with my soul.*
>
> *Horatio Spafford*

In the midst of life's greatest tragedies, Spafford still declared that his soul had peace. *It is well; it is well, with my soul.* The peace that passes understanding is exactly that—a peace that cannot be explained or even understood. It is peace with God regardless of circumstance because of the cross. It is a hope for eternity. In Spafford's grief, he had eternal hope to be reconciled with his Savior, Jesus, and rejoined with all of his children. In that hope, he found peace.

During those times when chaos reigns, it would seem impossible to have peace. Yet, the result of trusting God regardless of circumstance is *peace that passes understanding.* It is a deep *knowing* that everything has passed through the hand of God, so if God allows it, there is a purpose even in our pain.

This peace from Heaven is a release of anxiety in exchange for God's abiding presence. We rest in His arms knowing that everything on earth is temporal, including our sin and suffering. One day we will reach the heavenly shores where we will see our Savior face to face. With the Apostle Paul, who endured horrific suffering, we can proclaim:

> *For this light momentary affliction is preparing for us an eternal weight of glory beyond all comparison, as we look not to the things that are seen but to the things that are unseen. For the things that are seen are transient, but the things that are unseen are eternal (2 Corinthians 4:17-18 ESV).*

No matter what comes, we can proclaim that it is well with our soul—for our soul has been redeemed by the blood of Jesus because of His great love for us. In this deep love of God we find peace.

Further Investigation

Song: "It Is Well with My Soul," by Horatio Spafford

Bible Passage: Philippians 4:5-9

Memory verse: *The Lord is at hand; do not be anxious about anything, but in everything by prayer and supplication with thanksgiving let your requests be made known to God. And the peace of God, which surpasses all understanding, will guard your hearts and your minds in Christ Jesus (Philippians 4: 5b-6 ESV).*

Reflective activity: Memorize five verses that promote peace in your soul.

Prayer:

God of Peace,

With a heart of thanksgiving I give you praise for the peace that you offer amidst any circumstance. Though I grieve and mourn as I walk this earth, I have a deep abiding trust that you are sovereign and that you are in control of all things. I know that everything you allow in my life has a purpose. Though I may not understand your ways, I trust your heart of love. I pray that you will envelop me with your cloak of peace. Help me to trust you no matter what happens. Holy Spirit, please fill me with yourself so that I reflect your peace in every situation. Amen.

Sing For Joy; Dwell in Thanks

"Do not be grieved, for the joy of the Lord is your strength."

(Nehemiah 8:10b ESV)

I sometimes wonder if all pleasures are not substitutes for joy.

-C.S. Lewis

What is joy? Is joy the pleasure found in the moments of life that are fleeting and glorious? Is it the tender surge of emotion felt when a baby, bathed and powdered, nestles into your arms just before bedtime? Is it the bubbling delight felt when watching giggling children catch fire flies while running barefoot through summer grass, green and soft? Is joy the contentment that lifts one's spirits while enjoying toasty fires, steaming tea, and the sharing of life's unexpected pleasures with a treasured friend?

These moments of happiness are merely tributaries of the deeper river of joy that runs through the souls of believers. The flow of the river of joy is not dependent on circumstance; it runs deep and cool, soothing heartaches, quenching pain, and washing away sorrow. The source of this river is the Holy Spirit who abides in believers of Christ Jesus. Joy from the Holy Spirit is magnified by gratitude, and it swells in the hope of eternity.

Joy emerges from even broken vessels. It is found in the hope of those who tread the valley of the shadow of death. It reverberates in the songs of praise offered from broken hearts. Joy is like the arcing of lightning that illuminates the darkest storm or the brilliant colors of light that splits open night with the dawn of hope. Joy arises from the soul that offers quiet praise when all seems lost; it is the cry of the heart that rests in the Giver of hope.

Joy in the Darkest Night

My headlights illuminated the road just ahead of me as I steered my car out of the hospital parking lot into the starless, winter night. The outer darkness seemed symbolic of my mood which was dark, cold, and depressed.

The grim news of my premature daughter's progress seemed like a black hole pulling all light of hope into its unknown depth of despair. A chest tube had been inserted into Taylor's delicate one pound, thirteen ounce body to rescue a collapsed lung. Her lungs were so underdeveloped that they already required a full respirator and one hundred percent oxygen. This grave report balanced precariously on other serious conditions already being constantly monitored: a hole in her heart, unstable blood pressure, and a digestive system so immature it could only receive one drop of milk at a time through a feeding tube.

Future issues also loomed. Every new trauma threatened Taylor's chance of survival. We were waiting on results from a brain scan; fifty percent of premature babies her size had brain hemorrhaging. Retinopathy of prematurity, a retinal disease, was also a common issue for preterm babies. When I had asked the doctor about the prospect of her future vision, his eyes searched mine compassionately. "One day at a time," he had counseled. "Eye disease is still down the road. We have enough to deal with today." He was right; I was overwhelmed with the negative medical information, and I felt my hope for the survival of this precious daughter disappearing into the black hole of despair.

"Lord, Taylor is three weeks old, and I have never held her," I poured out my heartaches to God, angry that my omnipotent Father had allowed all this pain. The Holy Spirit reminded me of a verse I had memorized earlier in the week. *The Lord is near to the brokenhearted and saves the crushed in spirit (Psalm 34:18 ESV).* There was no reason to hide my thoughts and emotions from my all-knowing Father; He knew my every word before one of them formed on my tongue.

Memories of my visits with Taylor haunted me as I headed toward my parents' home, our temporary residence due to its proximity to the hospital. All I could do to comfort Taylor was to open the portholes of the incubator and touch her fragile skin. Her entire hand would grasp onto my index finger, clenching it tightly. She would try to open her eyes, perhaps recognizing my voice. The bright lights of the hospital were too much for her; however, so she closed her eyes and simply held my finger tightly.

"I am reaching for you like Taylor reaches for me, Lord," I prayed. "Where are you? I just want you to hold me, to rock my soul. I am desperate to just cling to you. Is this how Taylor feels? Abandoned? Alone? I can't hold her physically because she needs the incubator, but that doesn't change my love for her. I know you are there, too, watching and loving." I tried to voice truth that I couldn't feel. Only darkness surrounded me. Despair was closing in.

"I don't know how to deal with depression. I feel like I am going crazy—like I will never be the same. I will never be happy again. Taylor's life will change me forever. If she dies, I will never get over it. My happiness is gone. I will never again be known as a joyful person." Tears rolled down my cheeks as I poured out my heart to God. Typically, I saw the blessings in life and counted the joys. Dark moods usually passed quickly, but not this time. This time the dawn never seemed to break. I was in endless night.

"I Choose Joy", Larnelle Harris's song on the radio broke my train of thought and spoke God's truth to my soul. Joy was a choice. I had to decide if I was going to let my circumstances ruin my life and affect my relationship with God. I felt stunned that the Abba Father would speak to me so directly through the words of this song. Banging on my steering wheel with my fist, I proclaimed, "I choose joy! I choose joy! I choose joy! By your strength, God, I choose joy."

As I wept on my way home that night, my soul searched for joy. I pondered the way my headlights illuminated the night and the road before me. God would show me the way a little bit at a time just as my headlights showed the road ahead of me but didn't illuminate all the way home. A bit of hope was beginning to break through. "I will walk with you, God, one step at a time. And on that journey, no matter what comes, I choose joy."

Making a proclamation of joy is much easier than living it out. Still, it was a first step of determination to look for the good that God was doing, to dwell in thanks, and to focus on blessing. My faith journey rounded a corner, and my focus shifted to gratitude for God's blessings:

1. God is with me no matter what.
2. God has seen me through this far.
3. Taylor is alive.
4. Taylor is at one of the best neonatal hospitals in the country.
5. God is a God of miracles.

My joy and trust in God were being rebuilt by focusing on truth and dwelling in thanks. The joy of the Lord would be my strength (Nehemiah 8:10).

Joy Despite Circumstance

The Book of Acts chronicles the ministry of Paul and Barnabas, men who experience joy despite hardship and persecution. Paul and Barnabas received mixed responses from the people who listened to their message about Jesus. Some listeners begged to hear more. Gentiles rejoiced and believed. In Antioch, almost the entire city gathered to hear the Word of the Lord that Paul and Barnabas preached. Many of the Jewish people; however, were filled with jealousy. They contradicted and reviled Paul and Barnabas.

Despite persecution, Paul and Barnabas spoke boldly, and the Word of the Lord was spreading throughout the entire region. Eventually, hostility toward Paul and Barnabas was incited to such a degree that they had to leave the district. As they shook off the dust from their feet as they left, *the disciples were filled with joy and the Holy Spirit (Acts 13: 52 ESV).*

How could the disciples have joy in the midst of persecution? The Holy Spirit of God filled them, and with the Spirit is eternal joy. Even in the uncertainty of their life, Paul and Barnabas remained faithful to God's call on their lives. They walked in joy by the Holy Spirit's power because their joy was not dependant on circumstance.

Rick Warren, the author of *The Purpose Driven Life,* has experienced joy in difficult times much like Paul and Barnabas did.

Warren says most people see life as peaks and valleys. The peaks are the joy-filled times of life and the valleys are the sorrowful times of life. Warren says he believes life is more like a set of railroad tracks. One side of the track is sorrow and the other side joy. We usually have both joy and sorrow in our lives at the same time.

Warren came to this conclusion when his book, *The Purpose Driven Life,* became a huge success at the same time his wife battled cancer. Warren concluded that we have to choose our focus. This doesn't mean that we don't feel our sorrows, but rather that we don't let our sorrows drown out our joys. Perhaps Warren has hit upon one of the secrets to joy in any circumstance. When the way seems dark and hopeless, we need to focus on giving thanks. The old-fashioned method of counting your blessings is founded in eternal truth.

Perhaps that is why Paul and Barnabas experienced joy in persecution. They focused on the Holy Spirit's presence, the salvation of many, and the blessing of being part of God's eternal plan. Philippians 4: 8 explains it like this: *Finally, brothers, whatever is true, whatever is honorable, whatever is just, whatever is pure, whatever is lovely, whatever is commendable, if there is any excellence, if there is anything worthy of praise, think about these things (ESV).*

Choosing joy is a process of taking our thoughts captive, focusing on our blessings, and abiding with Jesus through prayer and reading of His Word. This does not mean we ignore our pain; instead, we pour out our hearts to God in prayer and thanksgiving. When we focus on God's blessings: naming, counting, treasuring and savoring them until our soul is well-nourished with the joy of the Lord, our strength is renewed.

Joy and Contentment

The Apostle Paul's joy was focused heavenward; it was eternal, not temporal. Paul explained that he had learned to be content in every situation and circumstance, even hunger, abundance, and great need. Paul proclaimed with joy: *I can do all things through Christ who strengthens me (Philippians 4:13 NKJV).* Paul's joy rested in his trust. *And my God will supply every need of yours according to his riches in glory in Christ Jesus. To our God and Father be glory forever and ever (Philippians 4:19-20 ESV).*

Since Paul experienced hunger and need, his words cannot mean that we will never suffer want. God will supply what we need to accomplish His purposes. This doesn't mean that we will never face hardship, but rather that God will provide His strength and grace for every hardship we face; in that we find joy.

Joy is Merged with Praise and Thanks

Joy is not the same as happiness. Happiness is a state of being dependent upon circumstance. Joy is a deep abiding trust in the truth of God. Joy watches for the eternal good, the soul growth, and the glory of God. Joy is a result of walking with God intimately and resting in the knowledge of His character: God is good, loving, holy, and does all things for His glory and the good of those who love Him. Joy is not dependent on circumstance; it looks beyond the temporal to eternity, and there it focuses on praise and thanks.

Paul and Silas demonstrated joy in the midst of suffering. Attacked by the crowd and dragged before the authorities for preaching the gospel, the magistrates ordered that Paul and Silas be stripped, beaten with rods, and severely flogged. As they were cast into prison, the jailer was ordered to guard them carefully, so he put them in the inner cell and fastened their feet in stocks.

Paul and Silas responded to this abuse by singing and praying. Can you imagine the shock of the other inmates who were listening?

> *About midnight Paul and Silas were praying and singing hymns to God, and the other prisoners were listening to them. Suddenly there was such a violent earthquake that the foundations of the prison were shaken. At once all the prison doors flew open, and everyone's chains came loose. The jailer woke up, and when he saw the prison doors open, he drew his sword and was about to kill himself because he thought the prisoners had escaped. But Paul shouted, "Don't harm yourself! We are all here!"*
>
> *The jailer called for lights, rushed in and fell trembling before Paul and Silas. He then brought them out and asked, "Sirs, what must I do to be saved?"*

> *They replied, "Believe in the Lord Jesus, and you will be saved—you and your household." Then they spoke the word of the Lord to him and to all the others in his house. At that hour of the night the jailer took them and washed their wounds; then immediately he and all his household were baptized. The jailer brought them into his house and set a meal before them; he was filled with joy because he had come to believe in God—he and his whole household (Acts 16: 25-34 NIV).*

Though beaten and abused, Paul and Silas had inner joy. It is difficult to know if their joy was the cause or the result of their praise. Did they receive joy because they prayed and gave thanks, or did they give thanks in prayer because they had joy? Perhaps prayer and thanksgiving are bound to joy in an unending circle of praise. One thing is certain, fighting the battle through prayer and praise resulted in an outpouring of Heaven's power.

Paul and Silas sang to express their joyous praise and thankfulness. Music is known as the language of the soul. It is the universal language that communicates through melody the words we cannot find. The Spirit uses music to unleash the emotions pent up in our soul, allowing us to pour out our heart to God in relief and refreshment. Music joyfully assists us in praise and worship.

Like Paul and Silas, we must learn to focus on thanksgiving and praise regardless of our circumstance. This allows our hearts to rest in joy, the strength that propels our perseverance. *...the joy of the Lord is your strength (Nehemiah 8:10 ESV).*

God was the source of Paul and Silas's joy. When we are in despair, we focus on our Creator, like the author of the following psalm did: *Then I will go to the altar of God, to God my exceeding joy; and upon the lyre I shall praise You, O God, my God. Why are you in despair, O my soul? And why are you disturbed within me? Hope in God, for I shall again praise Him, the help of my countenance, and my God (Psalm 43:4-5 NASB).* Despite our feelings of despair or lack of hope, we must praise the one who saves us and abides with us moment by moment. We tune our hearts to thanks and praise, the tools that uncap the deep, inner spring of joy.

Joyful Praise Brings Victory

Victory is usually a result of joyful praise and prayer. Certainly this was true for Paul and Silas when their prayer and praise preceded an earthquake that led to the salvation of souls and the glory of God. King Jehoshaphat also learned to lead the victory in joyful praise. Jehoshaphat had singers lead out his army of troops into battle. Jehoshaphat commissioned them to *sing to the Lord and to praise him for the splendor of his holiness (2 Chronicles 20:21 NIV).* The singers proclaimed God's glory as they led the army. *"Give thanks to the Lord for his love endures forever."* As they began to sing and praise, the LORD *set ambushes against the men of Ammon and Moab and Mount Seir who were invading Judah, and they were defeated (2 Chronicles 20:21b-22 NIV).* Praise and thanks led the battle in victory.

We, too, will find victory in the joy of praise and thanks. While every outcome might not be as we like, the battle for our soul will be victorious through Jesus Christ, our Lord. Singing praises from the heart works miracles. It weaves truth into every fiber of our thought; helps us surrender our will to the one who knows best, and encourages us to hope in a future that is secure in Jesus. Singing praise and giving thanks to God is a miraculous balm that soothes the aching soul. Thanks and praise kindle joy, and joy overflows in praise and thanks, an eternal praise that reaches from our heart to the throne of God.

Rejoice in God

Psalm 89: 11-18 NASB

The Heavens are Yours, the earth also is Yours;
The world and all it contains, You have founded them.
The north and the south, You have created them;
Tabor and Hermon shout for joy at Your name.
You have a strong arm;
Your hand is mighty, Your right hand is exalted.
Righteousness and justice are the foundation of Your
throne; Lovingkindness and truth go before You.
How blessed are the people who know the joyful sound!
O LORD, they walk in the light of Your countenance.
In Your name they rejoice all the day,

And by Your righteousness they are exalted.
For You are the glory of their strength,
And by Your favor our horn is exalted.
For our shield belongs to the LORD,
And our king to the Holy One of Israel.

How blessed are the people who know the joyful sound of praise! God's joy radiates on the faces of those who trust Him. We shout for joy in the name of the one who has created it all. He is strong and mighty, and His throne is the very foundation of righteousness and justice. He is the author of love and truth, and how blessed are the people who know this truth. Joy comes when we praise the Lord.

Sometimes you just know a person loves God because her countenance radiates joy. Before you meet her or know anything about her, you have this sense that she walks with Jesus because joy radiates out of her soul and lights up her countenance.

A nurse at my mother-in-law's nursing home is like that. She wears a bandana around her head; she is a cancer patient. Despite her obvious struggles, I suspected she belonged to Jesus before she introduced herself to me. Her kindness to those in her care was extraordinarily tender, patient, and thoughtful. She smiled and paused for a few minutes to listen to the stories of those on the threshold of eternity, those aged and frail patients whom most people ignored. One day, in a sweet tone, she introduced herself to me, and within moments she also shared her love for Christ. In the midst of her own struggles, she ministered joy to others.

This kind of joy comes from a deep sense of well-being. All will be well. God is sovereign and in control. We have hope, so we should rejoice!

While I was going through chemotherapy treatments, I loved to sing on the worship team. I never wanted to miss a Sunday of praising God with my church family. This rejoicing time was always a special time to remember that my future was full of glory and hope because no matter how much time I had left on earth, I had Heaven in my future. I remember feeling the Holy Spirit fill me in special ways during those months. Joy would take over; my entire being would tingle with excitement. Truth settled in my soul: God is good; I belong to Him; all will be well.

This didn't mean I wouldn't wrestle with fear or struggles, but underneath was an abiding sense of joy. When fear threatened, I would sing or recite Scripture. One of my favorite thoughts was, "I am His and He is mine. Nothing can separate me from His love."

God guarded my heart with joy in the night. Instead of waking and thinking of cancer, I would wake with a song in my head. Time after time I would wake singing songs of praise in the middle of the night. One day I came across a verse that explained this strange occurrence of waking to music. *By day the Lord commands his steadfast love, and at night his song is with me, a prayer to the God of my life (Psalm 42:8 ESV)*. The Holy Spirit was helping my soul respond with praise instead of worry. Instead of waking to think of cancer, I woke to dwell on God.

A week after chemotherapy ended, I went to a Newsboys concert. It was a celebration time. Near the end of the concert, we sang together, "Glory, glory, hallelujah, He reigns." God's joy flooded me with the truth of this phrase. God held the future. He reigned, and in this knowledge I could sing with all of my heart, "Glory, glory, Hallelujah!" As a gift of celebration, colored confetti was dumped from the ceiling of the convocation center; it danced in the currents of air all across the auditorium. Those few moments of victorious celebration were logged forever in my memory as moments of joyous trust in the God of my future. No matter what the future held, my God reigned!

That night of celebration at the Newsboys concert, I was overwhelmed with the amazing love of God. When we abide in the love of God, we have joy. God himself is the source of joy, and when we rest in His love; our joy will overpower our circumstance. The Apostle John explains how abiding in God's love brings joy:

> *As the Father has loved me, so have I loved you. Abide in my love. If you keep my commandments, you will abide in my love, just as I have kept my Father's commandments and abide in his love. These things I have spoken to you, that my joy may be in you, and that your joy may be full (John 15:9-11 ESV).*

God alone is the source and reason for our joy. We wait in hope for the Lord; He is our help and our shield. In Him our hearts rejoice; for we trust in His Holy name (Psalm 33:20-21 NIV). Joy gives us the strength to get through each day. This joy, founded in the presence of God, is eternal. *In Your presence is fullness of joy; In Your right hand there are pleasures forever (Psalm 16:11b NASB).* No matter what we face on earth, we know it is temporal, and we have eternal pleasures with God, forever.

Joy Through Others

Sometimes God uses other people in our lives to inspire joy. God's people are the hands and feet of Jesus, and these ministering saints are often dispensers of joy. Spending time with those we love, an aptly spoken word of encouragement, an act of service, a small gift, or a simple smile or hug are encouragements that lift others. Joy is contagious.

The Apostle Paul experienced the joy that others bring:

> *For when we came into Macedonia, we had no rest, but we were harassed at every turn—conflicts on the outside, fears within. But God, who comforts the downcast, comforted us by the coming of Titus, and not only by his coming but also by the comfort you had given him. He told us about your longing for me, your deep sorrow, your ardent concern for me, so that my joy was greater than ever (2 Corinthians 7:5-7 NIV).*

Paul makes it very clear that God uses people as messengers of joy, and in fact he credited God with sending Titus to comfort him. Paul did not hide his depression, but he acknowledged that God had seen his sorrow and sent Titus to cheer him.

Focusing on the joy of the company of others can help us when circumstances are most difficult. We focus on *living in the now* with those near us. We offer thanks for the people in our life and for all they mean to us, for joy rises on the wings of gratitude.

Who for the Joy Set Before Him

Jesus endured the cross by focusing on the joy set before Him. He looked to eternal joy. *. . . who for the joy that was set before him endured the cross, despising the shame, and is seated at the right hand of the throne of God (Hebrews 12:2 ESV).* God calls us to this same joy. Throwing off everything that hinders us and the sin that easily entangles us, we run the race set before us with endurance. Jesus is our focus. Our eyes are on Him as He stands at our finish line. Focused on Him, we run straight and true for we have joy set before us. When our focus is eternal, we do not lose heart nor grow too weary to go on. We finish the race God has set before us in the strength of joy.

While we run this race, we remember that the Book of James tells us to have joy, even in trials, because God has a plan for our good, even in our pain. Joy is not dependent on circumstance; it is a wellspring of gratitude for all that God has done and for all that He will do in the future. Joy is akin to hope which trusts in God no matter what.

God loves to turn our mourning into dancing (Psalm 30:11-12). We know that all of our sorrows will be banished when we reach the eternal shore. *Weeping may tarry for the night, but joy comes with the morning (Psalm 30:5b ESV).* Until we reach eternity's shore, life will have pain, but we rest in the hope that one day God will turn our mourning into dancing. As we wait for that day of eternal joy, we abide with Jesus moment-by-moment. With the psalmist we proclaim: *. . . for you have been my help, and in the shadow of your wings I will sing for joy (Psalm 63:7 ESV).*

When we find joy ebbing away, we focus on our blessings. Even in despair, there are things for which to be grateful. Be detailed in the counting of the little blessings of life. Ponder them; dwell on thanks. Joy gives birth to thanks, and thanks gives birth to joy in an endless circle of praise and gratitude to God. The greatest blessing of all is God himself: our Redeemer, our Rock, our Shelter, and our eternal home. In this we have fullness of joy.

Further Investigation

Song: "I Choose Joy," by Larnelle Harris

Bible Passage: James 1:1-4

Memory Verse: *"Do not grieve, for the joy of the Lord is your strength." (Nehemiah 8:10 ESV).*

Reflective question: Is it possible for joy and sorrow to co-exist? Share your thoughts with another person.

Prayer:

God of Eternal Joy,

    Because you are God, I can sing for joy no matter what my circumstance. I will hide under the shelter of your wings until the trouble has passed, for you are my comfort and strength. Just as Jesus focused on the joy set before Him, I look forward to the joy set before me in Heaven with you. One day I will see you face to face. On that day my mourning will forever be turned to dancing. In this joy and hope I take strength to persevere in this race for your kingdom and your glory. Fill my heart with your songs of praise even in the dark night of my soul, and may I give you glory and thanks forever. Amen.

Hope

This hope we have as an anchor of the soul, a hope both sure and steadfast...

Hebrews 6:19 NASB

Faith goes up the stairs that love has made and looks out of the windows which hope has opened. *–Charles Spurgeon*

"If the Lord calls me home before I see you again, rejoice!" This has been my mother-in-law, Ardith's, charge for ten years.

When she first began reciting this, tears would stream down my cheeks, but I would force a smile. "I'll be glad for you," I would whisper.

She'd wipe my tears, "Don't be sad," she'd continue. "This is what I want. This is what I have been waiting and hoping for my entire life. The day I see Jesus face to face will be my day of victory. You rejoice!"

I would nod, but in my heart I knew that rejoicing would not be my initial reaction. As the years have passed, though, and I have watched Ardith's body continue to fail, I know that on the day the Lord calls her home, I will rejoice through the tears because while life truly is a vapor that quickly vanishes, we have hope. Eternal life waits on the other side.

Ardith quoted the words of the Apostle Paul who wrote to the Corinthians about his hope for a new body. Paul explained that while our outer body is decaying; our inner soul is being renewed day by day. Though Paul suffered physically, he knew his suffering was temporal. Paul explained:

> *For we know that if the tent that is our earthly home is destroyed, we have a building from God, a house not made with hands, eternal in the Heavens. For in this tent we groan, longing to put on our heavenly dwelling, if indeed by putting it on we may not be found naked. For while we are still in this tent, we groan, being burdened—not that we would be unclothed, but that we would be further clothed, so that what is mortal may be swallowed up by life. He who has prepared us for this very thing is God, who has given us the Spirit as a guarantee.*
>
> *So we are always of good courage. We know that while we are at home in the body we are away from the Lord, for we walk by faith, not by sight. Yes, we are of good courage, and we would rather be away from the body and at home with the Lord. So whether we are at home or away, we make it our aim to please him (2 Corinthians 5:1-9 ESV).*

Ardith focuses on the hope of eternal life. Similar to the way the Apostle Paul encouraged the Corinthians, Ardith reminds us that though her body is frail and failing, she has the hope of a new body. She looks forward to the day that her mortality is swallowed up by life. That life is eternal; it will be a life with no more sorrow, pain, or suffering. So in hope, Ardith courageously waits for the day, the glorious day, that she will see Jesus face to face. Ardith's hope in Christ is an anchor for her soul.

Hope is an Anchor for the Soul

In the storms of life that rage around us, our souls search for a place to anchor. There is a Rock to keep us steady, sure, and firm despite the crashing waves of sorrow or the blustering winds of despair. When we cast our anchor of hope into the rock that is Jesus, our hope is steadfast and immovable even in the gales of life. There we anchor until the storms of life pass, and we can clearly see the heavenly shore.

When our hope is anchored in Christ, we may declare like the psalmist: *Why are you in despair, O my soul? And why have you become disturbed within me? Hope in God, for I shall yet praise Him, the help of my countenance and my God (Psalm 42:11 NASB.)*

Despite our pain, hope allows us to give thanks and to praise God in any circumstance because His sovereignty reigns over all (Psalm 103:19), and His purposes are always for the good of His children and the glory of His name. Hope paves the way to praise. *But as for me, I will hope continually, and will praise You yet more and more (Psalm 71:14 NASB).*

Hope sustains us in our waiting times. It allows us to trust in God's timing for He knows what is best for our soul. God is never slow about keeping His promises, but patiently waits for those who will call upon His name (2 Peter 3:9). As the psalmist declares, we wait in hope for God alone. *For God alone, O my soul, wait in silence, for my hope is from him (Psalm 62:5 ESV).* His timing is always perfect, though our earthly minds may not understand His ways.

As we anchor ourselves in Jesus, we exult in the hope of the glory of God. Everything that God allows has purpose to mold us into the image of Christ for the glory of His name. Hope encourages us to keep our eyes focused on Jesus and the eternal joy set before us (Hebrews 12:2). When we do this, even life's difficulties produce hope. The Apostle Paul explained:

> *More than that, we rejoice in our sufferings, knowing that suffering produces endurance, and endurance produces character, and character produces hope, and hope does not put us to shame, because God's love has been poured into our hearts through the Holy Spirit who has been given to us (Romans 5:3-5 ESV).*

In our troubles, we rest assured that our hope will not disappoint. The Holy Spirit's seal is His earnest, guaranteeing that which is to come, and in this hope our soul rejoices.

Lamentations Quelled by Hope

Focusing on Scripture and remembering the character of God increase hope. We must focus our thoughts on truth instead of letting our minds be dragged along in worry or despair. The prophet Jeremiah was comforted with remembrances of God's character which gave him hope for the future.

> *This I recall to my mind, therefore I have hope. The Lord's lovingkindnesses indeed never cease, for his compassions never fail. They are new every morning; great is Your faithfulness. "The Lord is my portion," says my soul, "therefore I have hope in Him." The Lord is good to those who wait for Him, to the person who seeks Him (Lamentations 3:21-25 NASB).*

We have hope because Jesus is the embodiment of everlasting love. The Apostle Paul declared:

> *Who shall separate us from the love of Christ? Shall tribulation, or distress, or persecution, or famine, or nakedness, or danger, or sword? . . . No, in all these things we are more than conquerors through him who loved us. For I am sure that neither death nor life, nor angels nor rulers, nor things present nor things to come, nor powers, nor height nor depth, nor anything else in all creation, will be able to separate us from the love of God in Christ Jesus our Lord (Romans 8:35 & 37-39 ESV).*

The love of God is the very substance of our hope.

Hope in God's Plan for His Glory and Our Good

We all have days when hope seems to vanish. Gloom settles in like fog and confuses our thoughts with its darkness. Even in our most difficult times, however, God has a purpose in all that we go through, and in this we have abundant hope. Our God reigns! King David summarized it like this: *Let the heavens be glad, and let the earth rejoice, and let them say among the nations, "The Lord reigns." (1 Chronicles 16:31 ESV).* When we remember that God is in control of everything, our circumstances are seen in the light of His glory and grace. Hope dispels despair.

Jeremiah is known as the weeping prophet, and even though he sent a letter to the Israelites predicting much hardship, he also offered encouraging hope to the Israelites who had been taken into captivity by

Nebuchadnezzar. Jeremiah starts the letter by proclaiming that it was God who sent them into exile from Jerusalem to Babylon, even though it was done at the command of Nebuchadnezzar. Since God reigns over all, His hand is even in the hardships we suffer.

Jeremiah encouraged the captives to live full lives in Babylon. He told them to build houses and live in them, plant gardens and eat their produce, marry, have children and grandchildren, and seek the welfare of the city where they were exiled; for their exile would last seventy years. Seventy years is a lifetime; for the Israelites that meant a lifetime of captivity.

Yet in the midst of this heart breaking prophecy, Jeremiah reminded the Israelites that God was working for their good. *"For I know the plans that I have for you," declares the Lord, plans for welfare and not for evil, to give you a future and a hope (Jeremiah 29:11 ESV).* Jeremiah charged the Israelites to have hope because even their captivity was part of God's plan for them, and God's plans were for the good of their souls. Jeremiah prophesied the good that God would accomplish: *Then you will call upon me and come and pray to me, and I will hear you. You will seek me and find me, when you seek me with all your heart (Jeremiah 29: 12-13 ESV).* God will do what it takes to draw us to himself because of His great love for us.

God's ways are higher than our ways. When we do not understand His ways, we have hope in His loving kindness and compassion. He knit us in our mother's womb, and He will sustain us to the very end. King David declared his hope in a God that sustained him from birth: *For you, O Lord, are my hope, my trust, O Lord, from my youth. Upon you I have leaned from before my birth; you are he who took me from my mother's womb. My praise is continually of you (Psalm 71:5-6 ESV).* Each of us has a purpose in our own generation (Acts 13:36). Our times are in his hands (Psalm 31:15). We have hope in a plan that transcends earth's sorrows to Heaven's joys.

Hope in the Outcome

When we trust that God allows all things for His glory and the good of those who love Him, we have hope in the outcome of every situation. We hope in an omnipotent God. This all powerful God is the God of miracles. He can move mountains. Hope remembers that nothing is impossible with God.

Hope recognizes that outcomes are affected by prayer. Hope takes action through prayer because God ordains prayer to be the way that we are included in His work. *The effective prayer of a righteous man can accomplish much (James 5:16b NASB).* Prayer is a pathway of hope that travels to the throne of God. As we pray in faith, hope believes that even the impossible is possible with God.

Shadrach, Meshach, and Abed-nego had hope in the God who has no limitations. King Nebuchadnezzer was enraged that these young men of God would not bow down to worship his golden image. Irrational with fury and pride, Nebuchadnezzer was determined to throw them into a fiery furnace. Just before their seemingly hopeless fate, Nebuchadnezzer questioned and ridiculed their God. . . . *who is the god who will deliver you out of my hands (Daniel 3:15 ESV)?*

Full of hope in the Almighty, these three brave warriors for God were not intimidated. They declared, *"If this be so, our God whom we serve is able to deliver us from the burning fiery furnace, and he will deliver us out of your hand, O king. But if not, be it known to you, O king, that we will not serve your gods or worship the golden image that you have set up." (Daniel 3:17-18 ESV).*

The hope and faith of these brave young men rested in God alone. They believed that God would rescue them from the fire. But even if He did not, they would not worship false gods. They had hope and trust in God's plan for their life, and they knew that ultimately God would rescue them—either on earth—or through death into glory.

Centuries later, Peter wrote a letter to early Christians that encouraged them to also have hope in God despite their fiery trials. He reminded them that trials are allowed for the good of their souls. Peter explained, *Therefore, let those also who suffer according to the will of God entrust their souls to a faithful Creator in doing what is right (1 Peter 4:19 NASB).* Even in our suffering, we can be assured that God hears us. If God allows pain, it has a purpose. In this truth we hope.

Hope in God's Promises

Let us hold fast the confession of our hope without wavering, for he who promised is faithful (Hebrews 10:23 ESV). When we begin to lose hope, we must remember our faithful God. His promises are sure. He does everything He says He will do. He is the same yesterday, today, and forever. We have hope in the faithfulness of God who says He will never leave us nor forsake us. Our God declares His love and compassion for His children, and He promises to work all things for the good of those who love Him.

Abraham had hope in the faithfulness of God; he knew God would keep His promises. The Book of Romans says: *In hope against hope he believed . . . (Romans 4:18a NASB).*

Despite circumstances that seemed impossible, Abraham hoped in a God who is faithful to keep every promise. God had promised Abraham a son. Years had passed and Abraham and his wife, Sarah, were very old, yet God had not given them the promised son. Though all evidence suggested that God's prophecy would never be fulfilled, Abraham hoped.

> *Without becoming weak in faith he contemplated his own body, now as good as dead since he was about a hundred years old, and the deadness of Sarah's womb; yet, with respect to the promise of God, he did not waver in unbelief but grew strong in faith, giving glory to God, and being fully assured that what He had promised, He was able also to perform (Romans 4:19-21 NASB).*

God did give Abraham a son, just as He had promised. They named him Isaac.

Why would God wait until Abraham and Sarah were many years past child-bearing age to give them their promised son? God's timing is not always our timing. God was glorified through Abraham's faith and this miracle of life. Abraham's story of miraculous hope and the fulfillment of God's promise has encouraged believers for thousands of years. God knew what He was doing even though His ways were unconventional! God never makes a mistake. His timing is perfect. We have hope in a faithful God.

Years later, God called Abraham to sacrifice Isaac, his son, for whom he had waited so long. Abraham's faith and hope were again prominent. God had promised that Isaac's offspring would become a nation. Abraham had hope and faith to believe that even if he sacrificed Isaac, God would bring him back to life because God had promised, and God was faithful. Abraham had hope in God's promise . . . . *through Isaac your descendants shall be named (Genesis 21:12b NASB).* The Book of Hebrews explains that *He* (Abraham) *considered that God is able to raise people even from the dead . . . (Hebrews 11:19a NASB).*

God never required Abraham to sacrifice Isaac; He provided a ram for the sacrifice. Abraham's hope and faith in God were steadfast and proved his love for God.

Even when we do not understand God's ways, or when His promises seem impossible to fulfill, we can hope in a God who has been faithful always. *Now faith is the assurance of things hoped for, the conviction of things not seen (Hebrews 11:1 ESV).* Even in times of near despair, we can hope in a God who is ever faithful. Every promise will be fulfilled in its time.

Hope in the Valley of the Shadow of Death

The eternal hope that we have protects us from the ravages of the fear of death. When it is time for God to call us to our heavenly home, He will be with us in the Valley of the Shadow of Death (Psalm 23:4). King David declared in hope: *Surely goodness and mercy shall follow me all the days of my life, and I shall dwell in the house of the Lord forever (Psalm 23:6 ESV).*

Hope helps us set our minds on the things above even as we face death. During our last days on earth, may we have the grace to proclaim with the Apostle Peter:

> *Blessed be the God and Father of our Lord Jesus Christ! According to his great mercy, he has caused us to be born again to a living hope through the resurrection of Jesus Christ from the dead, to an inheritance that is imperishable, undefiled, and unfading, kept in Heaven for*

you (1 Peter 1: 3-4 ESV).

Hope for Eternity

Hope believes that life conquers death through Jesus Christ. Time on earth is like the beginning point of a geometrical ray that stretches endlessly into eternity future. This eternal future holds untold joy, hope, love, and peace. No matter how difficult life on earth is, it is temporary. For those who have put their faith and hope in Jesus, our struggle will end the moment we meet Jesus face-to-face. In all of Job's loss, he had hope for eternity. *If a man dies, will he live again? All the days of my struggle I will wait until my change comes." (Job 14:14 NASB).*

The Bible says that God's eternal perspective of time is different from our earthly view. To God, one thousand years is like a day, so in Heaven's perspective, all of life on earth is just a speck of living compared to infinite eternity. God grieves with us when we lose a loved one, but He promises that our parting is temporary if we belong to Him. Truly life on earth is like grass that withers. God hears our cries of grief and knows our breaking hearts, but He also knows our grief is temporary. It is then that He whispers to our soul reassurances of reunion in eternity.

For those who hope in Christ, death is not the end. When believers die, we hope to see them again. We do not grieve as those who have no hope (1 Thessalonians 4:13). Perhaps our loved ones who have gone to eternity before us will become part of the great cloud of witnesses described in Hebrews 12:1. Perhaps they are surrounding us and cheering us on as we run the race with endurance to the finish line.

Several years ago, four people who were dear to me passed from earth into eternity in a relatively short period of time. As I grieved, I tried to think of time from an eternal perspective. I imagined God saying, "Welcome home! The rest of your family will be home for lunch." For if one thousand years is like a day, then all of earth's time is like just a few hours to God.

The years since my loved ones have been gone seem like just a blink of time. Memories of them keep them near to me. In a few more blinks, I will be home with them and all the others I have loved and lost that have gone before me to the arms of Jesus.

Heaven's joys will exceed our hope. Our Heavenly Father is creating a new Heaven and a new earth, and God himself will dwell among us (Revelations 21:3):

> . ... *He will wipe away every tear from their eyes, and death shall be no more, neither shall there be mourning, nor crying, nor pain anymore, for the former things have passed away." And he who was seated on the throne said, "Behold, I am making all things new."(Revelation 21:4-5a ESV).*

This new Heaven and earth will be far more glorious than we can think or imagine. Life's earthly joys are only a foreshadow of Heaven. The Apostle John describes Heaven in the Book of Revelation as a city having the glory of God with brilliance like a costly stone of crystal-clear jasper. The city is pure gold, like clear glass, and its foundation is adorned with precious stones. Each gate of the city is a single pearl, and the glory of God illuminates it for its lamp is the Lamb. Its gates shall never close. The river of the water of life flows from the throne of God and of the Lamb. There shall no longer be any curse. In this new Heaven and earth, we will reign forever and ever (Revelation 20 and 21).

Heaven is a place of rejoicing and gladness. Peace, joy and love reign for there will no longer be any curse. . . . *no more shall be heard in it the sound of weeping and the cry of distress (Isaiah 65:19b ESV).* Even the animals will dwell in peace during the Millennial Kingdom. *"The wolf and the lamb shall graze together; the lion shall eat straw like the ox, and dust shall be the serpent's food. They shall not hurt or destroy in all my holy mountain," says the Lord (Isaiah 65:25 NASB).*

Because we have this hope laid up in Heaven, we can have the strength to endure whatever comes. Life on earth is temporary, and one day those found in Christ will have eternal joy. In the meantime, we *press on toward the goal for the prize of the upward call of God in Christ Jesus (Philippians 3:14 ESV).* We strive to honor God as we walk this sin scarred earth. We desire to be counted worthy of our calling. By God's grace, we press on to fulfill every desire for goodness and the work of faith with power *so that the name of our Lord Jesus may be glorified in you, and you in him, according to the grace of our God and the Lord Jesus Christ (2 Thessalonians 1:12 ESV).*

Further Investigation

Song: "Hope Now," by Addison Road

Bible Passage: 1 Peter 1:3-9

Memory Verse: *Why are you in despair, O my soul? And why have you become disturbed within me? Hope in God, for I shall yet praise Him, the help of my countenance and my God (Psalm 42:11 NASB).*

Reflective question: Why is hope such an essential part of our faith?

Prayer:

God of all hope,

 You are a faithful God, and your promises are true. My hope is in you. I know that you are always with me; you will never leave nor forsake me. Thank you for the promise of eternal life through my Savior, Jesus Christ. What a glorious hope to know that the suffering on earth will soon be over, and in Heaven there will be no more sorrow, no more death, no more sickness, no more pain. As I wait for the days of eternal joy and peace in your presence, help me to run the race with endurance for your glory and praise. Amen.

Final Note to the Reader

Dear Reader:

The seed for this book was sown surrounding the birth of my daughter, Taylor. Much of her story you have read interspersed throughout the pages of this book. Four months of complete bed rest followed by three and a half months of her hospitalization created abundant time to search my soul and to cry out to God.

When we brought Taylor home, her medical issues continued. Her asthma, resulting from respirator-damage to her delicate, immature lungs, was so severe that we could hear her wheezing across the room. We could not take her out of the house for a year. Her eye disease had damaged her retinas, so she began wearing glasses at fourteen months of age. Imagine trying to find glasses hidden by a fourteen-month-old! She certainly couldn't tell us what she had done with them. Taylor's early years were not easy years, but our difficult days were faith building days where we learned to trust the Lover of our soul in deeper ways. Those days also had much happiness in them. Taylor abounded with irrepressible laughter; she was effervescent and charming. Our hearts overflowed with gratitude to God even in the difficulties.

God's Word became my lifeline during those years. I would crave it like a baby craves milk. Morning, noon, and evening I would find God in the pages of the Bible, his love letter to me. There He would comfort, encourage, and tell me of His great love.

I began writing this book at that time, but during the chaos of raising children, it was shelved. Fifteen years passed, and during those years I had many health struggles. I was diagnosed with a spinal nerve tumor that required an eight hour surgery which left me with permanent nerve damage, loss of strength in my dominant hand, and chronic pain that was quite severe for two years. Eighteen months after that surgery, I was diagnosed with breast cancer. I underwent a mastectomy and chemotherapy. The medications that were required for my cancer treatment caused macular holes in both eyes, requiring eye surgery and leaving permanent visual impairment.

When I returned to writing this book that had long been on my heart, I found the tone had completely changed. What had begun as a rather light-hearted journaling of my walk with God during difficult times became a joyous, but broken, praise of a journey with God through the darkest night.

This book is intended to be an encouragement to those who are broken-hearted, discouraged, or doubting. Hang on to Jesus! Leap that wall of doubt, fear, anger, or whatever it is that attempts to keep you from God! By God's grace, your faith can be strengthened even in your pain.

You are a treasure so valued by God that he would give up everything just to have you with Him. And that is exactly what Jesus did. He left the glories of heaven to come to earth to take the penalty for our sin.

Do you know how deeply you are loved? Do you feel loved? You are so loved that God knows your every thought and how many hairs are on your head. You are loved with an everlasting love that stretches from eternity past to eternity future. God's love is unending, unbounded, and immeasurable.

Jesus is the lover of your soul. Do you know Him? He is not far from any of us. He holds His arms open wide waiting for you to come to Him. He longs to gather you into His arms; He will shelter you from the storms that rage around you. Won't you come to Him? Surrender all of your heartaches and sorrows; pour out your heart to him like water. Come to the Savior who came to earth because of his great love for you.

The path is simple, and yet so difficult that it can only be followed by the grace, strength, and guidance of the Holy Spirit. Jesus' simple call to the disciples was, "Follow me." The gospel message is clear. Repent and believe. *For all have sinned and fall short of the glory of God*

(Romans 3:23 NASB). Tell Him all of your heartaches and failings. He already knows; you cannot hide from Him. Agree with God for your need for a Savior, not just the Savior of the world, but the Savior of you! His desire is to have intimate fellowship with you. He longs to walk with you daily. He is the Rock to which you anchor your hope.

When we believe in Christ, He sends his Holy Spirit to abide in us. The Spirit offers comfort in every trial, peace for anxiety, and hope for despair. He will carry us all along earth's journey, through joy and despair. He promises to never leave us nor forsake us. He will be with us across deserts of despair, through pain so great we can barely gasp breath, and He will guide us through the valley of the shadow of death. He will sing for joy over us in our moments of uncontained praise, unexplainable peace, and when in hope against hope we believe. He will guide us to the very shores of Heaven where God waits with outstretched arms. *Precious in the sight of the Lord is the death of his godly one (Psalm 116: 15 NASB).*

For those of you who already know Him as your personal Lord and Savior, be encouraged to run this race with perseverance. Keep your eyes on the prize which is Jesus himself. Focus on the joys and details of blessing in every day. Live in the moment you are given with hearts full of gratitude and praise. Remember who God is and all that He has done. Wait for His perfect timing. Rest in His loving kindness. Sing for joy. Dwell in thanks. Seek after Him with all of your heart, mind, soul, and strength. Trust the one who is the lover of your soul. And the God of peace will be with you.

Dear reader, remember that you are loved, and you are never alone. The Creator of the Universe is closer than your very breath. You are precious in His sight, and He loves you.

You may contact Julie Kloster or read her blog at her website: JulieKloster.com. She can also be contacted through Facebook at JulieKloster, writer.

Bibliography

Alcorn, Randy. *Heaven*. Tyndale House, 2004.

Chan, Francis. *Crazy Love: Overwhelmed by a Relentless God*. Colorado Springs, CO: David C. Cook, 2008.

"Charles W. Colson: Founder," Prisonfellowship.org, 2011, http://www.prisonfellowship.org/why-pf/leadership/founder.

Chisholm, Thomas O., and William M. Runyan. "Great Is Thy Faithfulness". Carol Stream, IL: Hope Publishing Company, 1923.

"Christian Quotes on Relationship with God Index Page 2," dailychristianquote.com, http://dailychristianquote.com/dcqrelationshipgod2.html.

"C.S. Lewis Quotes – Brainy Quotes," BrainyQuote, Bookrag Media Network, 2001-2011, http://www.brainyquote.com/quotes/quotes/c/cslewis132782.html - 21k -.

Elliot, Elisabeth. *Quest for Love: True Stories of Passion and Purity*. Baker, 2002, paperback.

ESV MacArthur Study Bible. Crossway Books and Bibles, 2010.

Gaither Vocal Band. "We Have This Moment Today."Allthelyrics.com, 2002-2010, http://www.allthelyrics.com/lyrics/gaither_vocal_band/we_have_this_moment_today-lyrics-318634.html.

"It Is Well With My Soul – A Hymn and It's History", biblestudycharts.com, http://www.biblestudycharts.com/A_Daily_Hymn.html - 50k -.

Jeremiah, David. *A Bend in the Road*. Thomas Nelson, 2002, paperback.

Lehman, Frederick M., and Claudia L. Mays. "The Love of God". *Songs That Are Different, Vol. 2, 1919*. Cyberhymnal.org, 2007, http://www.cyberhymnal.org/htm/l/o/loveofgo.htm.

Lehman, Frederick M. *History of the Song, "The Love of God"*, 1948.

Cyberhymnal.org, 2007, http://www.cyberhymnal.org/htm/l/o/loveofgo.htm.

Lillenas, Haldor. "Wonderful Grace of Jesus", 1918, Cyberhymnal.org, 2007, http://www.cyberhymnal.org/htm/w/o/wondergj.htm - 5k -.

Lotz, Ann Graham. *Why?: Trusting God When You Don't Understand.* Nashville, TN: W Publishing Group, a division of Thomas Nelson, Inc., 2004.

MacDonald, George and Rolland Hein. *Life Essential: The Hope of the Gospel.* Vancouver: Regent College Publishing, 2004.

"Memory," Stanford Encyclopedia of Philosophy, first published Tue March 11, 2003; substantive revision Wed. Feb 3, 2010, John Sutton, 2010, http://plato.stanford.edu.entries/memory.

Newton, John. "Amazing Grace". Allthelyrics.com, 2002-2010, http://www.allthelyrics.com/lyrics/john_newton/amazing_grace-lyrics.

"Quote by Amy Carmichael,"goodread.com, Goodreads Inc, 2012. http://www.goodreads.com/quotes/show/312034 - 27k.

"Quotes by Charles H. Spurgeon," goodread.com, Goodreads Inc, 2012. http://www.goodreads.com/quotes/show/69721 - 86k -.

Piper, John. *Desiring God, Revised Edition: Meditations of a Christian Hedonist.* Multnomah Books, 2011, paperback.

Rose, Darlene Deibler. *Evidence Not Seen: A Woman's Miraculous Faith in the Jungles of World War II.* New York: HarperSanFrancisco, 1988.

"Thomas Merton – BrainyQuote," BrainyQuote, Bookrag Media Network, 2001-2011, http://www.brainyquote.com/quotes/quotes/t/thomasmert117537.html.

Warren, Rick. *The Purpose Driven Life: What On Earth Am I Here For?* Zondervan, 2011, paperback.

Wilson, Ralph F. "Amazing Grace, The Story of John Newton, Author of American's Favorite Hymn", Joyful Heart Renewal Ministries, Joyfulheart.com, http:www.joyfulheart.com/misc/Newton.htm.

Julie Kloster is a freelance writer, teacher, and speaker. She has written over thirty Bible studies for *CHRISTIANBIBLESTUDIES.COM*, a division of *CHRISTIANITY TODAY;* devotionals for Standard Publishing; and she is the author of The Eternal Truths of Narnia, a Bible study on The Chronicles of Narnia. She lives in Sycamore, Illinois with her husband and three daughters. You can find her blog, ministry opportunities, and speaking topics at juliekloster.com or on Facebook at juliekloster, writer.

Made in the USA
San Bernardino, CA
12 December 2012